THE LIVING
WHITE HOUSE

TEXT BY LONNELLE AIKMAN

Published by the
WHITE HOUSE HISTORICAL ASSOCIATION
with the cooperation of the
NATIONAL GEOGRAPHIC SOCIETY
Washington, D. C.

THE LIVING WHITE HOUSE

by Lonnelle Aikman
*Produced by the National Geographic Society
   as a public service*
Gilbert M. Grosvenor, *President and Chairman
   of the Board*
Robert L. Breeden, *Executive Adviser to the President
   for Publications and Educational Media*
PREPARED BY
Donald J. Crump, *Editorial Director*
Mary Ann Harrell, *Stylist*
Jody Bolt, *Art Director*
Geraldine Linder, *Illustrations Research*
Margaret B. Klapthor, Curator Emeritus, Division of Political History, National Museum of American History, Smithsonian Institution; and Dr. Richard L. Watson, Jr., Professor Emeritus of History, Duke University, *Text Consultants*
STAFF FOR THE NINTH EDITION:
Elizabeth W. Fisher, *Editor*
Jane H. Buxton, *Consulting Editor*
Lori Davie, *Picture Editor and Researcher*
Cynthia B. Scudder, *Designer*
Judith E. Rinard, *Revision Writer*
Jolene Blozis, *Indexer*
George V. White, *Director,* and Robert W. Messer, Vincent P. Ryan, *Managers,* Heather S. Guwang, *Production Project Manager; Manufacturing and Quality Management*

White House staff members who assisted in preparing this edition: Susan Porter Rose, *Deputy Assistant to the President and Chief of Staff to the First Lady;* Anna Perez, *Press Secretary to Mrs. Bush;* Rex Scouten, *Curator;* Betty C. Monkman, *Associate Curator;* David Valdez, Janet McConnell, and Barbara Henckel, *Photographic Office;* Maria Eitel Sheehan, *Deputy Director of Media Relations*

OPPOSITE: *George and Barbara Bush pass between flags of the United States and of the President as they enter the Rose Garden on April 5, 1989. There they honored the National Teacher of the Year, and the President signed a paper sending new legislation for education to Congress.*

COVER: *Greenery of the south lawn frames the White House in its 18-acre parklike setting.*
DAVID P. JOHNSON, NATIONAL GEOGRAPHIC STAFF

ENDPAPER: *Glowing gas jets turn the White House to gold as guests arrive for a January reception in 1886, during President Grover Cleveland's first term.*
LIBRARY OF CONGRESS

OVERLEAF: *Resplendent in scarlet tunics, the Marine Band performs on the South Portico terrace as Members of Congress and their families await the arrival of President Jimmy Carter at a 1978 picnic on the south lawn.*
KARL SCHUMACHER, THE WHITE HOUSE

MICHAEL SARGENT, THE WHITE HOUSE

CONTENTS

CAROL T. POWERS, THE WHITE HOUSE

In the White House Library, an attentive audience listens as Barbara Bush reads aloud—an activity she loves and encourages in all caregivers. For more than ten years Mrs. Bush has focused her volunteer activities on literacy and reading; she is "convinced that poor reading skills are linked to so many of our other social problems. . . ."

FOREWORD

WITH THIS BOOK, *The Living White House*, George and I take pleasure in sharing with you a portrait of life in this historic house, which began in 1800 when John and Abigail Adams became its first residents. The White House is a symbol of America's history and government, as well as a very real home for the families that have lived here.

In this house, babies have been born, and brides married at festive occasions, from the beautiful wedding of Teddy Roosevelt's daughter Alice to Tricia Nixon's lovely Rose Garden ceremony.

Here, also, children of all ages have laughed, played, and romped with their pets on the White House lawn. Benjamin Harrison's young grandson, Benjamin, once raced out onto Pennsylvania Avenue in a cart pulled by a pet goat named His Whiskers. Later, Caroline Kennedy rode her pony, Macaroni, on the south lawn, and Amy Carter played in her tree house there. Today, our own grandchildren delight in exploring this great home and learning about history firsthand.

Living here is a special privilege and joy. We can admire the beautiful rooms and furniture, have the pleasure of using historic china of earlier Presidents, and share the excitement of welcoming so many distinguished guests, including heads of state from around the world.

The White House is also a wonderful setting to highlight causes, including making America more literate. As Lady Bird Johnson once said, it gives you "a bully pulpit . . . a chance to do something for your country that makes your heart sing."

Most important of all, we truly enjoy sharing this house with you. For although it is often called The President's House, it really belongs to the American people.

I hope that as you read *The Living White House*, published by the White House Historical Association and produced by the National Geographic Society, its stories will give you a new appreciation for this historic national monument. I would like to acknowledge the enduring achievement of the book's author, the late Lonnelle Aikman, whose work lives on in this, the ninth edition.

Barbara Bush

Barbara Bush

1

HAIL TO
THE CHIEF

THE WHITE HOUSE is part of every American's national inheritance. As the office and home of the President, it is the one place toward which citizens look for leadership from the man they themselves have chosen to act for all. No other elected official is so directly accountable to them. Their problems are his problems; his home is theirs.

John Adams, the first Chief Executive to live in the White House, once wrote, "People of the United States! You know not half the solicitude of your presidents for your happiness and welfare. . . ."

"I never forget," said President Franklin Delano Roosevelt in one of his famous fireside chats, "that I live in a house owned by all the American people and that I have been given their trust."

The Executive Mansion has been a focal point of government and a barometer of the political, economic, and social state of the nation ever since it was first occupied in 1800, a decade after Congress had set up the country's permanent Capital in the fields and forests beside the Potomac River. It has known the tramp and flames of enemy invaders; victory celebrations and economic depressions; high-fashion weddings and the somber pageantry of state funerals.

Unlike the ornate and monumental palaces of Europe's royal past, the porticoed White House stands today with unpretentious charm amid green and rolling grounds in the heart of Washington. Separated by a

Rolling out the red carpet, President and Mrs. Bush come to the North Portico of the White House to welcome Egypt's President Hosni Mubarak and his wife, Suzanne, to the Bush Administration's first formal dinner, on April 4, 1989.

high iron fence from swirling traffic and hurrying pedestrians, it still may look to a traveling Briton "like an English clubhouse," as the famous novelist Charles Dickens described it after a visit with President John Tyler in 1841.

Such an appearance befits the headquarters of the Chief Executive of a Republic that came into being in defiance of the power and pomp of reigning kings.

The first four Presidents who lived in the house—John Adams, Thomas Jefferson, James Madison, and James Monroe—earned their credentials for the nation's highest post by serving the cause of American independence and helping to hammer out the Constitution.

George Washington, though "Father of His Country" and "first in the hearts of his countrymen," was the only President who never slept in the White House. For he ended his service as Chief Executive and died before the Federal government was moved from Philadelphia to the village Capital named in his honor.

On a visit to the Federal City, George Washington inspects the unfinished President's House with architect James Hoban. Below, houses top a hill in Georgetown (at left) and line the Potomac River waterfront of Washington in a romantic engraving published in 1801.

E VEN SO, WASHINGTON left the indelible mark of his own dignity and good taste on this 18th-century building with its magnificent view. He selected its site and gave his prestigious approval to the simple, harmonious design for the mansion submitted by Irish architect James Hoban in a democratically open competition.

From the beginning the "President's House"—the name Washington preferred—was destined to be a stage for events that marked the progress of the nation from fewer than a score of states stretched along the Atlantic seaboard to a pre-eminent world power reaching into the Pacific Ocean. Here President Jefferson devised a plan, soon after his inauguration, to purchase the French-owned port of New Orleans and thus keep the Mississippi River outlet open to American trade.

The move would have far-reaching consequences, which Jefferson was quick to appreciate after Napoleon suddenly offered to sell not only the port but also the entire wilderness empire reaching from the Mississippi River deep into the West.

Known as the Louisiana Purchase, the treaty was negotiated with Napoleon's representatives in Paris by Jefferson's special envoy, James Monroe, and the American minister, Robert R. Livingston. Its ratification by Congress—despite Jefferson's own doubts about the deal's constitutionality—virtually doubled the territory of the young Republic at a bargain price of $15,000,000. It also underscored the practical need for the Lewis and Clark Expedition that Jefferson had already launched to explore the region.

To the President's House in 1829 came tough, flamboyant Andrew Jackson. "Old Hickory" was the first man to reach the top executive office from the open frontier beyond the Appalachians. His overwhelming Presidential victory in 1828 clearly demonstrated the new political power of a growing and more democratically based electorate, and alerted the aristocratic statesmen of the East to a fact of life: Henceforth

national leadership must be shared with the people of the West.

During his first few years in the Presidential saddle, Jackson rode head on into a furious controversy growing out of intense sectional rivalry between northern and southern states, and foreshadowing the eventual bloody test of the Union's very survival.

The long dispute came to a climax in 1832 when South Carolina nullified a Federal tariff on foreign imports, levied to aid northern manufacturers. From the White House the President issued a warning proclamation. In his statement Jackson called South Carolina's claim of states' rights, coupled with threats of secession, a "fatal doctrine" whose success would mean "our present happy Constitution was formed . . . in vain. . . ."

Putting muscle behind his words, he sent ships to command the port of Charleston and made it clear that he would call out Federal troops if necessary. Armed confrontation seemed imminent, but Jackson's firm stand, followed by Congress's reduction of import taxes in general, eased tension. The crisis passed.

Three decades later, Abraham Lincoln bore the burdens and heartbreak of the "irrepressible conflict" of the Civil War in the vortex of the struggle—the White House. Through bitter military reverses and petty partisan politics—in the face of cruel criticism and cartoons picturing him as a clown and a devil—he held together the frayed bonds of union until the nation could again be united.

"I think of Lincoln, shambling, homely, with his strong, sad, deeply furrowed face, all the time," Theodore Roosevelt wrote a friend after he, too, came to live and work in this house of historic memory. "I see him in the different rooms and in the halls . . . he is to me infinitely the most real of the dead Presidents."

But the fascination the building holds for most Americans has its roots in more than association with the great men who helped create the United States.

T HE WHITE HOUSE, whose long-popular name was not officially inscribed on the Presidential letterhead until Theodore Roosevelt's time, stands as a living symbol of the nation's power and prestige. The office of the Chief Executive is the keystone of the government. Flanked by the Congress and the Supreme Court, it is the central theater of action in which national gains are won and defended.

In a world of dire emergencies and instant communications, the White House has become a focal point of the fierce, incessant searchlight of global attention. To meet the demand to know what goes on here, some 100 men and women reporters and photographers—from newspapers, magazines, television, and radio—regularly cover activities of the President and First Lady. Nearly 1,600 others have credentials and attend special events, such as visits of foreign officials.

Since World War II, an ever lengthening procession of foreign leaders has come to 1600 Pennsylvania Avenue to confer on global problems.

Abigail Adams, welcomed at right by her husband, John, arrives at the still-unfinished White House. The couple lived here only four months before Adams's term expired in 1801. Above, granddaughter Susanna helps supervise as a servant hangs wash in the East Room.

PAINTING BY GORDON PHILLIPS, 1966 (ABOVE); DRAWING BY LOUIS S. GLANZMAN, 1970

Thomas Jefferson observes a black-billed magpie and a prairie dog, brought 4,000 miles in 1805 from the winter camp of the Lewis and Clark Expedition. He sent them to Charles Willson Peale of Philadelphia, who had established a museum in Independence Hall. Thanking Jefferson, Peale wrote: ". . . every thing that comes from Louisiana must be interresting to the Public."

Usually dignitaries are also formally entertained at the White House, and an invitation to attend such a function is highly coveted. Certainly a state dinner to honor a visiting head of government or a reigning monarch is one of the most glamorous of White House affairs.

At the white-columned North Entrance, the President and his wife greet their guests of honor and escort them to the second-floor Yellow Oval Room. There they meet with other top-ranking guests, such as the Secretary of State. Meantime, a hundred or so other guests are arriving at the East Entrance. Leaving their wraps in the East Wing, they ascend the marble stairway to the state floor.

There, they are presented with cards explaining seating arrangements and conducted to the East Room by social aides, officers chosen from the Armed Forces. On their way, they walk across the Entrance Foyer, where the red-coated Marine Orchestra—the President's own since 1801—is playing a lively popular tune. As they enter the room, another social aide announces each new arrival.

Suddenly the aides snap to attention and the music changes to the stirring strains of a march. The President and his wife, with their guests of honor, are descending the grand stairway from the family floor. At the foot of the steps, the group pauses for official photographs. Then, to the roll of drums in the familiar "Ruffles and Flourishes" salute, followed by the triumphant march "Hail to the Chief," the President and his party move along the red-carpeted corridor to the East Room.

Forming the official receiving line, the host and hostess greet everyone in protocol order and present them to the honored visitors. Finally, the President offers his arm to the ranking woman guest and leads the way to the State Dining Room, followed by the First Lady on the arm of the ranking gentleman, and the rest in turn.

The public does not have to wait long to learn details of the dinner. Late-night television newscasts and next-day newspapers often carry pictures and stories on the guests, menu, and entertainment. To obtain such information and to add firsthand descriptions to their coverage, a few White House reporters have long been permitted to attend the after-dinner entertainment and to chat with the guests.

As another aid to the news media, President Johnson had an electronic system installed so that reporters assembled in another room could hear the traditional toasts exchanged by the two heads of state. More recently, some foreign leaders have arranged for video coverage of the dinners for live broadcast or later use in their home countries.

D URING HIS FIRST two and a half years in office, George Bush was host at the White House for 16 state visits. His guests came from around the globe: from Europe and Africa; from Asia and South America. Among the most recent were South Korean President Roh Tae Woo, Nicaraguan President Violeta Chamorro, Brazilian President Fernando Collor, and Great Britain's Queen Elizabeth II. Since his inauguration, President Bush has consulted with more than 320 world leaders, including 92 presidents, 6 kings, 5 queens, 65 prime ministers, 1 emir, 1 chancellor, 7 princes, and 131 foreign ministers.

In another and more intimate aspect, the White House occupies a unique place in American life. As the home of Presidential families for more than 190 years, it has represented, by democratic extension, the homes and families of all Americans.

Since the early Federal period of John and Abigail Adams, this "First Home" has mirrored America's everyday domestic fashions and attitudes, household decor, furnishings and utensils, in ways that would have been unthinkable to the followers of social and political traditions practiced in Europe's great state residences.

More than that, the personal and family life in the White House has given to this center of national power and influence a warm, human note of common experience and understanding.

President and Mrs. John Adams, for instance, were far from happy in November 1800 when the time came to move into the damp and incomplete Executive Mansion being readied in the raw little Capital. Only four months remained of Adams's single term, and Mrs. Adams was dismayed at the condition of their temporary home.

The house was "made habitable," she wrote her daughter in Massachusetts, but the main stairs were not yet up, not a single apartment had been finished, and bells for summoning the servants were "wholly wanting to assist us in this great castle."

Abigail's rheumatism came back, too, in the chill caused by a scarcity of logs for the many fireplaces. ". . . shiver, shiver," she complained, ". . . surrounded with forests, can you believe that wood is not to be had, because people cannot be found to cut and cart it!"

The most famous housekeeping problem Mrs. Adams faced, however, still makes an amusing subject for conversation at White House parties. Since there was, she said, "not the least fence, yard, or other convenience" available outside, she hung the Presidential laundry to dry in the huge, unfinished East Room, destined to become the most elegant of the state chambers used in entertaining.

Beginning with John Adams, whose personal discomfort in the new White House was matched only by the political vicissitudes of his outgoing administration, each succeeding President has led two lives while in office—his own and his country's.

Thomas Jefferson, a scholar and a gentleman, confounded Federalists who predicted that his belief in equality would bring disorder and destruction. Instead, he maintained an atmosphere of personal moderation and a social style of fine living and intellectual interests that belied the crude surroundings of the wilderness Capital.

To relax from the heavy responsibilities of leadership in a young Republic starting out in a world of hostile monarchies, the long-widowed President turned to hobbies he had enjoyed at his Monticello home. He played his fiddle, experimented with familiar and rare plants, and taught his pet mockingbird to peck food from his lips and to hop up the stairs after him.

The White House reflected the quiet happiness of James and Dolley Madison and the generous hospitality presided over by the genial Dolley before they were burned out of the mansion in the War of 1812.

Washington Irving, after attending one of Mrs. Madison's popular Wednesday-evening receptions, described her as "a fine, portly, buxom dame" and "poor Jemmey . . . a withered little apple-John." Others pointed out the couple's mutual devotion and admiration. Dolley once wrote that the sensitive, studious President was her "darling little husband." He said a conversation with her always brought a bright story and a good laugh, as refreshing as a long walk in the park.

AMONG MORE RECENT PRESIDENTS, Woodrow Wilson often appeared to outsiders as a perfect example of the austere, erudite professor. Yet within his close and affectionate family before the death of his wife, Ellen, he was a jaunty, fun-loving man, fond of group singing, impersonations, and limericks.

When he married again, after a period of deep despondency, President Wilson found with his second wife, Edith, a renewal of happiness he had never expected to know again. Without her "love and care . . . I

Near the end of the War of 1812, fire set by British troops roars through the White House, August 24, 1814. Dolley Madison (diorama) salvaged what she could, including the Gilbert Stuart portrait of George Washington (far right).

don't believe he could live," Mrs. Wilson's social secretary, Edith Benham, wrote in the dark days after the strain of his stubborn but futile League of Nations campaign had left him a paralyzed, broken man.

The Dwight D. Eisenhowers established at the White House the most permanent home they had known during the far-ranging career of the popular general with the broad smile. "I have seen my grandchildren growing up in these historic rooms," Mrs. Eisenhower wrote. "Here my son and daughter-in-law have shared our family evenings."

Life with the Carters reflected the easy atmosphere found in many small southern towns, such as their native Plains, Georgia. A story that made the Capital rounds early in 1977 revealed something of their ways. Picking up a telephone soon after she arrived at the White House, Mrs. Carter asked to be connected with Jimmy. "Jimmy who?" came the response from the operator.

President Reagan and his wife, Nancy, introduced a bit of California's casual life-style, plus a touch of elegance, to the mansion.

President George Bush and his wife, Barbara, bring to the White House a warm atmosphere that emphasizes traditional family values. A close couple, they delight in their family of five children and twelve grandchildren, who visit frequently. Friends and official guests alike are welcomed to their home with an easy graciousness that reflects their years of diplomatic service as well as the informal life-styles of Texas and the Maine coast.

O VER THE YEARS, the public image projected by every President and his family has been part fiction and part reality, part personal and part official. Until 1902, when Theodore Roosevelt built the West Wing to separate his office from his living quarters, all families shared the Executive Mansion with the public, which was freely admitted to ask favors, to seek interviews with the President, or just to shake his hand.

When Herbert Hoover and his wife, Lou, invited all comers to the traditional New Year's Day reception in 1930, 6,000 people appeared. By 1932, the annual open house and handshaking had become such an ordeal that the Hoovers decided to be out of town the following year. The custom was never revived.

The President's House, as the people's property, has remained open in selected areas under regulations permitting as much inspection as possible without interfering with the family's privacy or with official functions. From Tuesday through Saturday, sightseers—some with babies in arms—line up outside the iron fence enclosing the 18-acre estate. Visitors now number a million and a half a year.

Surging through the East Gate, they walk through the Ground Floor Corridor and up a marble stairway to find an astonishing and colorful spectacle. Here, five state rooms, one opening into another, spread a brilliant pageant, from the white-and-gold East Room, through the Green, Blue, and Red Rooms, to the State Dining Room.

President Andrew Jackson salutes—and strengthens—the Federal Union, threatened by talk of secession. At a Washington banquet on April 30, 1830, backers of a plan to nullify a Federal tariff opposed by South Carolina gave 24 toasts full of states' rights ideas. Jackson's simple reply rallied public opinion to his position: "Our Federal Union— It must be preserved."

DRAWING BY PAUL CALLE, 1967

Furnished in late 18th- and early 19th-century styles—original pieces and faithful reproductions—these rooms are much like stage sets, with portraits of past Presidents and First Ladies enhancing the scene. Life-size paintings of George and Martha Washington dominate the capacious East Room. The Gilbert Stuart likeness of the first President, obtained in 1800, is the oldest remaining possession of the house.

It was this priceless portrait that Dolley Madison saved when she fled before British troops approaching Washington during the War of 1812. The President had joined the defending forces in Maryland. Mrs. Madison, in a letter to her sister, explained how she saved the painting. "Our kind friend, Mr. Carroll, has come to hasten my departure," she wrote, "and is in a very bad humor with me, because I insist on waiting until the large picture of Gen. Washington is secured, and it requires to be unscrewed from the wall. This process was found too tedious . . . I have ordered the frame to be broken and the canvas taken out; it is done."

Many other portraits of those whose lives are forever interwoven with memories of this building hang in the state rooms. Their attire, from knee breeches and hoopskirts to modern dress, recalls the many eras the house has known, as Presidents moved in to shape and be shaped by events, and to leave on the American character the imprint of their philosophy and words. Jefferson wrote, ". . . our liberty can never

19

be safe but in the hands of the people themselves." Lincoln said, "with malice toward none . . ." and showed compassion that might have helped heal the wounds after the fratricidal war if he had survived.

"Speak softly and carry a big stick," was a favorite motto of "Teddy" Roosevelt, who launched the building of the Panama Canal, won a formidable reputation for "trust-busting," and sent 16 battleships of the United States Navy on parade around the world.

A long list of memorable phrases emerged during the White House years of Franklin D. Roosevelt, the only President elected to four terms. Best remembered perhaps are the "New Deal," "economic royalists," "arsenal of democracy," and "the Four Freedoms."

Considered as a group, the 40 men who have taken on their country's toughest assignment reflect the geographic and cultural diversity that is the hallmark and strength of this nation. Virginia, "Mother of Presi-

Abraham Lincoln, tallest man present, welcomes guests near a White House doorway during a "Grand Reception" in January 1862. Mrs. Lincoln nods a chilly greeting to Secretary of the Treasury Salmon P. Chase and his daughter, Kate (center). Kate had earned Mrs. Lincoln's dislike by promoting her father's campaign for the Presidency.

dents," claims eight as native sons. Ohio has contributed seven; Massachusetts and New York, four each; North Carolina, Texas, and Vermont, two apiece. California, Illinois, Iowa, Kentucky, Missouri, Nebraska, New Hampshire, New Jersey, Pennsylvania, South Carolina, and Georgia have each produced one President.

Together, the lives of these varied leaders support the democratic proposition that every native American, regardless of origin, has a chance to reach the highest position in the land. Abraham Lincoln was born in a log cabin, as were several other Chief Executives—an indication of humble beginnings that had a very potent political appeal to voters in frontier days.

The rollicking campaign of William Henry Harrison rolled to success in 1840 on a bandwagon bearing twin symbols of a log cabin and a barrel of hard cider, despite the fact that Harrison was not born in a log cabin

Troops of the Bucktail Brigade—Company K of the 150th Regiment of Pennsylvania Volunteers—seek the shade for

a cribbage game. The Bucktails—named for snippets of fur on their caps—guarded Lincoln during the Civil War.

but was a scion of Virginia aristocracy and had no special taste for cider.

As to education, Lincoln was self-taught, and Jackson's lack of academic learning was sometimes cited to embarrass him, while the Adamses—both father and son—were Harvard graduates, experienced in the diplomatic and social circles of Europe.

Andrew Johnson, who learned to read and write with his wife's help, was a tailor before he entered politics. Franklin D. Roosevelt came from a rich and patrician family of New York. John F. Kennedy, descendant of Irish immigrants, inherited drive and fortune from a father whose business acumen brought his family millions; and Richard M. Nixon was reared in Whittier, California, the second of five sons, in a modest Quaker home.

Gerald R. Ford grew up in Grand Rapids, Michigan, as the adopted son of a devoted stepfather—a small businessman struggling to survive the Depression of the thirties. Jimmy Carter graduated from the Naval Academy in 1946 but gave up a seagoing career to take over the family peanut farm after his father's death. Elected to the Georgia Senate, he

went on to serve as governor before becoming President. Ronald Reagan was the first professional actor to achieve America's highest political rank. Earlier, Reagan worked as a radio sportscaster, served in the U. S. Army Air Corps, and was twice elected governor of California.

George Herbert Walker Bush was born in Massachusetts and grew up in Greenwich, Connecticut, and Kennebunkport, Maine. After service as a Navy pilot in World War II, he married Barbara Pierce and graduated from Yale University before moving to Texas. There he worked in the oil business and was twice elected to Congress. George Bush later served as U. S. Ambassador to the United Nations, Chief of the U. S. Liaison Office in the People's Republic of China, and Director of the Central Intelligence Agency. He was the first sitting Vice President in more than 150 years to be elected President.

Eleven Presidents were former generals—from George Washington to Dwight Eisenhower. Warren Harding had been a newspaper publisher; Herbert Hoover had been an engineer. Several were teachers or college professors. At least 20 practiced law early in their careers; many

Amicable transfer of power, hallmark of the American system, keeps the government running smoothly. At Woodrow Wilson's inauguration in 1913, he and President Taft ride from the White House to the Capitol in a four-horse victoria. Above, on their last morning in the mansion in 1961, President and Mrs. Eisenhower bid farewell to staff members.

served as state officials, Members of Congress, and Cabinet officers.

Eight Vice Presidents rose to the Presidency on the death of incumbents; four of these—Theodore Roosevelt, Calvin Coolidge, Harry S. Truman, and Lyndon Johnson—went on to win another term on their own. Gerald R. Ford was the only Vice President to attain the office by the resignation of a Chief Executive. He replaced Richard M. Nixon, who left under threat of impeachment by Congress.

Another novel event in Presidential history occurred when William Howard Taft, following his defeat for a second term in 1912, was appointed by President Harding to be Chief Justice of the United States—the only man ever to serve in both high posts. Of the two, Taft preferred heading the Supreme Court. "I don't remember that I was ever President," he once remarked happily.

Others reacted in different ways to the executive burdens. "I enjoy being President," Theodore Roosevelt wrote to his son Kermit, "and I like to do the work and have my hand on the lever." John Quincy Adams remembered his years at the White House as "the four most mis-

President Nixon faces an array of cameras as he welcomes students on the White House lawn. The early-day amateur photographer above, with one of the first box cameras, took pictures of the Easter egg rolling on the grounds in 1889.

erable" of his life. Truman called the mansion "a great white prison."

"What is there in this place," cried James A. Garfield, who was hounded by office seekers, and who would finally be murdered by one, "that a man should ever want to get in it."

Yet there has never been a shortage of candidates for the position that Jefferson described as "a splendid misery," and Jackson found to be "dignified slavery." Coolidge dryly commented, when warned of the dangerous condition of the White House roof, that he presumed there were plenty of others willing to risk living under it.

In view of the frantic nature of many election campaigns, it is amazing that there has never been an interruption in the lawful exchange of masters at 1600 Pennsylvania Avenue. The nearest approach to such disruption occurred in 1877, after Rutherford B. Hayes lost the popular vote to his rival, Samuel J. Tilden, and neither candidate won the necessary majority in the Electoral College. With the opposing parties deadlocked, an Electoral Commission chosen by Congress decided in favor of Hayes. But Tilden's followers challenged the decision.

Because of the bitter dispute and because March 4, then the legal Inauguration Day, fell on Sunday, Hayes took the oath of office in a private White House ceremony on March 3 while attending a dinner given by outgoing President Ulysses S. Grant.

Few of the dinner guests were aware of the event when President Grant quietly led the other principals into the Red Room, where Hayes was secretly sworn in by Chief Justice Morrison R. Waite. The formal inauguration took place peacefully at the Capitol on Monday, March 5.

However placid the transfer of leadership, each new President inherited heavier and more complex duties and responsibilities as the nation grew from some five million people in 1800 to some two hundred and fifty million in 1990.

Behind the stately pillars of the Executive Residence, as in the inconspicuous East and West Wings where most official business goes on, many staff members help their chief meet his obligations, great and small. Their tasks include gathering information and receiving visitors, handling mail and documents, carrying on domestic routines, and preparing for a constant round of social and other activities.

E VEN THE museum-like state rooms are forever in use when not on public display. Though the press records official events held in these historic rooms, few people—other than those responsible for providing facilities and food—realize the extent and variety of the succession of social and working functions.

At three White House luncheons in 1982 and 1984, the Reagans celebrated the birthday centennials of former Presidents Franklin D. Roosevelt and Harry S. Truman and of former First Lady Eleanor Roosevelt.

Ceremonial affairs presided over by President and Mrs. Bush have included state dinners for Prime Ministers Bhutto of Pakistan, Andreotti of Italy, Hawke of Australia, Antall of Hungary, and Presidents Perez of Venezuela, Gorbachev of the Soviet Union, Walesa of Poland, and Aquino of the Philippines.

President Bush warmly toasted Corazon Aquino at dinner and recalled how she led her country's struggle toward a free society: "You . . . proved ballots are stronger than bullets." In his toast to Prime Minister Jozsef Antall, Bush remembered a barbed-wire piece of the Iron Curtain given to him on a visit to Budapest. He praised Hungary's "courageous decision to open its borders, unleashing a force that . . . eventually brought down the Berlin Wall."

A dinner for Queen Margrethe II of Denmark in February 1991, the first state dinner since the beginning of the Persian Gulf War, welcomed a longtime American ally. Noting that forces of both their countries were facing a common enemy in the gulf, Bush told the Queen that once again "we stand together."

The Bush Administration continues to meet its international obligations, with official dinners and working lunches. The most frequent entertaining, however, takes the form of large receptions. In February of

1989, an elegant white-tie reception, with a receiving line in the Blue Room, was held to honor the Washington Diplomatic Corps. Some 400 foreign ambassadors and their wives attended.

Other large White House receptions honor a wide variety of groups and have equally varied guest lists. Government officials, scholars, business leaders, scientists, artists, and athletes stroll through the five state rooms, chatting and admiring the furnishings.

An elegant workshop as well as a party setting, the East Room provides a backdrop for the President's press conferences, for swearing-in ceremonies, and for a variety of other special occasions.

Mrs. Bush, too, uses the state rooms to welcome spouses of visiting heads of state and other dignitaries and to highlight the work of many organizations, including the Leukemia Society of America, the Girl Scouts of the U.S.A., and Reading Is Fundamental. In May of 1989, Mrs. Bush held a luncheon for 100 literacy and education experts to launch the Barbara Bush Foundation for Family Literacy, an organization formed to help establish literacy as a value in every American family.

Whether they come for parties, work, or sightseeing, visitors find inscribed on the mantel of the State Dining Room a benediction and an expression of hope from the earliest days of the Republic. The words were taken from a letter written by John Adams on his second night in the building. Franklin Roosevelt had them cut into the mantel face so that all who passed might see:

"I Pray Heaven to Bestow
The Best of Blessings on
THIS HOUSE
and on All that shall hereafter
Inhabit it. May none but Honest
and Wise Men ever rule under This Roof."

Historic meeting at the White House in 1981: President Reagan joined three former Presidents— Ford, Carter, and Nixon (left to right). The three served as his emissaries to the funeral of Egypt's Anwar Sadat.

2

WHERE HOSPITALITY MAKES HISTORY

AT NO OTHER TIME OF YEAR is the White House more beautiful and festive than during the Christmas season, when it is decked with holiday finery. During the month of December 1990, more than 100,000 visitors toured the mansion to see the yuletide decorations. The dazzling display included 47 Christmas trees that glowed with 54,000 tiny lights, swags of fragrant greenery, arrangements of red, white, and pink poinsettias, fresh holly and flowers, and red-bowed wreaths at every window in the Executive Residence.

Tourists entering the Blue Room saw the official White House tree—a massive 18½-foot Fraser fir. Its decorative theme, Tchaikovsky's ballet *The Nutcracker*, was inspired by Mrs. Bush's love for the arts. Ornaments included 45 richly dressed porcelain figures created by White House florists, representing characters in the ballet, and 50 pairs of ballet slippers, one pair signed by Bolshoi Ballet company dancers.

In the East Room, visitors saw trees hung with velvet garlands, gold balls, musical instruments, and Florentine angels, as well as an 18th-century Italian crèche of carved wood and terra-cotta.

In addition to daytime tours, on certain evenings visitors could go through the state rooms, their way lighted by the flickering glow of red wax candles. More than 40 groups of carolers, hand-bell ringers, and other musicians took turns providing music for holiday visitors.

The holiday season is a time for sharing the White House with family, close friends, and other visitors. Barbara and George Bush greet their guests in the Blue Room beside the official White House tree, which nearly touches the ceiling.

Dancing at his son's wedding, February 25, 1828, John Quincy Adams steps to a lively Virginia reel with the bride, the former Mary Catherine Hellen. John— the only White House bridegroom among Presidents' sons—talks with his mother (below at left). The officiating clergyman, Dr. William Hawley, stands third from right against the wall. Eight years earlier, on March 9, 1820, he had presided at the wedding of Maria Hester Monroe (left), the first President's daughter to be wed in the White House. She married her cousin, Samuel Laurence Gouverneur, in a private ceremony. Officials and social leaders paid "visits of congratulations" at two evening receptions.

At other times of the year, the White House showcases other kinds of entertainment. President and Mrs. Bush continue the series of concerts titled *In Performance at the White House,* initiated by the Carters and broadcast over public television. Mrs. Carter had explained that the idea for this program "came about because Jimmy and I knew there were so many people who had never been to the White House. . . . We wanted all of America to enjoy the White House like we did."

A 1989 concert held in the East Room featured opera baritone Simon Estes and ragtime pianist Joshua Rifkin, among others.

Sometimes, too, entertaining in the Executive Residence literally reflects American history. In 1970 President and Mrs. Nixon commemorated George Washington's birthday by presenting the lively Broadway musical *1776,* by Peter Stone and Sherman Edwards. Based on the 1776 session of the Continental Congress in Philadelphia, the play recalled the struggle that raged before the divided delegates adopted the Declaration of Independence. Funny, tender, and serious by turns, it brought to life Thomas Jefferson, Benjamin Franklin, and John Adams, as actors spoke and sang their immortal words to lilting tunes.

F EW SETTINGS could be more appropriate for such a production. But then symbolism pervades the Executive Mansion. Whatever their personal style, no President and his wife can ever forget that they act as the nation's official host and hostess. Recognizing this, John and Abigail Adams required guests to show the kind of deference to the new Republic that subjects accorded rulers of monarchies abroad. During their short stay in the village Capital, the Adamses practiced the formal court etiquette adopted for a similar reason by President and Mrs. Washington in New York and Philadelphia.

In the upstairs oval room, hung with crimson draperies, Mrs. Adams remained regally seated to greet the town's leading citizens and foreign diplomats who attended the President's weekly levees, or receptions. By her side, dressed in black velvet coat and knee breeches, silver buckles and lace, John Adams bowed solemnly to arrivals, who then took designated seats around the wall.

Such formality went out the window when Thomas Jefferson became President. He emphasized, instead, his cherished ideals of equality and democracy. In his words, he "buried . . . levees, birthdays, royal parades," and replaced them with two main White House receptions, open to all, on New Year's Day and the Fourth of July.

Jefferson entertained Jérôme Bonaparte, Napoleon's youngest brother and future King of Westphalia, after that impetuous young man married the Baltimore belle, Betsy Patterson. Jefferson once invited his butcher to dinner. The man brought his son, explaining that the boy

Celebrating newfound political power, common folk unleash a fury of admiration ▷
for President Andrew Jackson during his inaugural reception in the White
House. "Old Hickory" quietly escaped the mob and spent the night at a hotel.

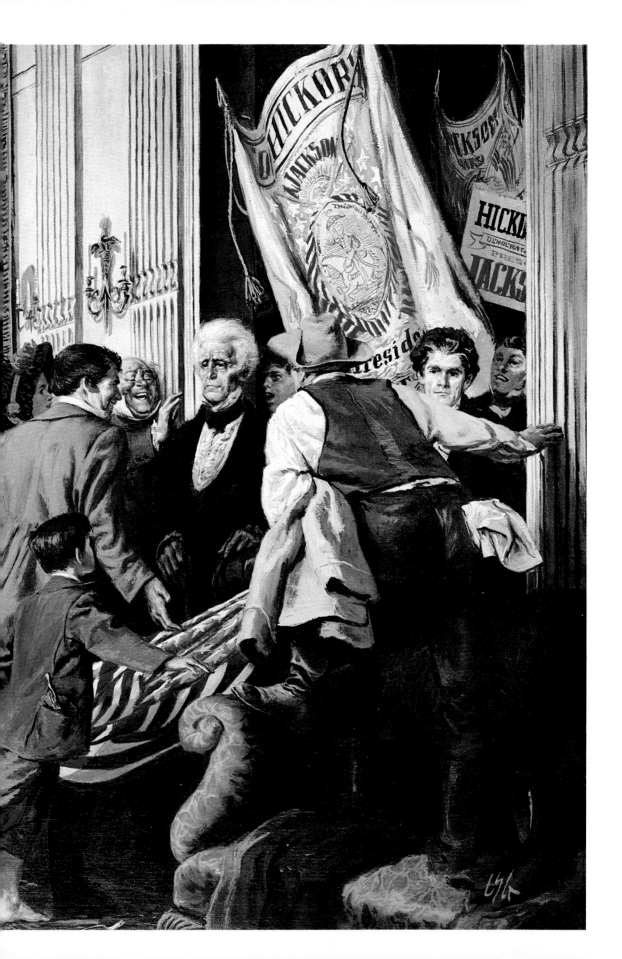

could use the place left by a guest who was ill. And the President made both feel welcome among the distinguished company.

His dislike for ceremony, however, only highlighted Jefferson's good manners and excellent taste. He served the finest wines and hired a French chef to prepare the most exotic foods. Around his small, informal table, he assembled charming women and the wittiest, most knowledgeable men to be found in the city or coming from abroad to visit the strange young Capital.

In learning and accomplishments, Jefferson himself was unique. His interests ranged from music and history to farming, astronomy, anthropology, and architecture. And it was this erudition that President John F. Kennedy referred to in his famous toast at a 1962 dinner honoring 29 Nobel Prize winners. His guests, said Kennedy, made up "the most extraordinary collection of talent, of human knowledge, that has ever been gathered together at the White House, with the possible exception of when Thomas Jefferson dined alone."

President Jefferson replaced the custom of bowing with the more democratic practice of shaking hands. The greeting proved so popular that no successor could abandon it, despite the painful pressure from thousands of hands embracing the privilege.

Slight James K. Polk, once described as the "merest tangible fraction of a President," found a way to avoid a painful grip. ". . . when I observed a strong man approaching," he said, "I generally took advantage of him by being a little quicker . . . seizing him by the top of his fingers, giving him a hearty shake. . . ."

Lincoln performed the task, in the words of an observer, "as though . . . splitting rails as of yore." On January 1, 1863, before signing the Emancipation Proclamation, he shook hands for three hours at the usual New Year's reception. Upstairs in his Cabinet room, he spread the official copy on the table, dipped his pen in ink, and paused.

"I never . . . felt more certain that I was doing right. . . ," he said, looking at Secretary of State William H. Seward. "But . . . my arm is stiff and numb . . . if they find my hand trembled, they will say, 'he had some compunctions.' But, any way, it is going to be done!"

Then, slowly and carefully, Abraham Lincoln wrote the bold signature that appears at the end of the document.

B ESIDES SHAKING HANDS with the public at special events, most Presidents regularly made themselves available for the ritual as recently as the time of Calvin Coolidge. White House doors were then opened for the purpose daily, just before lunch. Rather surprisingly, the taciturn New Englander thoroughly enjoyed the contact.

"On one occasion I shook hands with nineteen hundred in thirty-four minutes. . . ," Coolidge recalled in his autobiography. "Instead of a burden, it was a pleasure and a relief to meet people in that way and listen to their greeting, which was often a benediction."

No one ever took more delight in receiving people and making them

First envoys from Imperial Japan bow to President Buchanan and his Cabinet on May 17, 1860. Visiting to exchange ratifications of a commercial treaty, the Japanese presented their documents in a box earlier borne ceremoniously along Pennsylvania Avenue.

ILLUSTRATED LONDON NEWS, JUNE 16, 1860, LIBRARY OF CONGRESS, TINTED BY P. HALL BAGLIE (ABOVE); PERLEY'S REMINISCENCES

welcome than did vivacious Dolley Madison. Even before she became First Lady, she sometimes served as official hostess for the widowed Jefferson while James Madison was Secretary of State.

After she moved into the mansion in 1809, Dolley made the President's House the rallying point of Washington's fast-burgeoning social life. In "the blazing splendor" of her drawing room, as Washington Irving described it, were gathered, said another guest, "all these whom fashion, fame, beauty, wealth or talents, have render'd celebrated."

While "the great little Madison" met with his Cabinet, Dolley often entertained the wives at "dove parties." Taking no sides in political disputes of the day, she was cordial to Federalist and Republican leaders alike. To callers in general, she served refreshments of seed cake and hot bouillon in winter, punch in summer.

Perhaps compensating for the subdued dress of her Quaker girlhood, statuesque Dolley arrayed herself in rich silks and satins and accentuated her height with magnificent turbans, sometimes decked with ostrich plumes. Yet so obvious was her honest friendliness that everyone found her appealing, notwithstanding her exaggerated dress and man-

President Lincoln towers over his guest, Prince Napoleon (wearing sash), as Secretary of State William H. Seward cheerfully talks of victory only two weeks after the Union defeat at Bull Run, July 21, 1861. Beyond a flag-crowned Marine Band pavilion rises the uncompleted Washington Monument.

nerisms. " 'Tis here the woman who adorns the dress," said a contemporary commentator; ". . . in her hands the snuff-box seems only a gracious implement. . . ."

In 1812 Mrs. Madison arranged the first nuptials held at the White House—the wedding of her handsome widowed sister, Lucy Payne Washington, to "the estimable & amiable" Supreme Court Justice, Thomas Todd. Even then, according to one observer, dashing Dolley innocently held the spotlight, "looking every inch the queen."

Then suddenly, brutally, the mansion's "Golden Age," as some called the Madison era of entertaining, came to an end. The War of 1812 had broken out five months before Madison's reelection. It dragged on, mostly in sea engagements far from Washington, until the electrifying news struck the Capital on a hot August 23, 1814, that the British had landed troops in Maryland.

Gathering members of his Cabinet, President Madison galloped off early the next day to join the American forces near Bladensburg, Maryland. As the battle began, valiant little "Jemmy" sat astride a horse within sight of the front line, while British rockets exploded near him.

FRANK LESLIE'S ILLUSTRATED NEWSPAPER, LIBRARY OF CONGRESS, TINTED BY P. HALL BAGLIE

Meantime, Mrs. Madison remained at the White House, watching through a spyglass for her husband to return, "ready at a moment's warning to enter my carriage and leave the city," as she wrote her sister in an hour-by-hour letter.

"I am still here within sound of the cannon!" she added at three in the afternoon. "Two messengers covered with dust, come to bid me fly; but I wait for him."

Friends finally persuaded Dolley to leave and escorted her across the Potomac into Virginia, where Mrs. Madison eventually would join the President. Her flight came none too soon. Having scattered the Bladensburg defenders, the British troops marched into Washington that evening and put the torch to the White House, the Capitol, and other public buildings. A torrential thunderstorm saved the city from devastating destruction, but the Executive Mansion was reduced to a blackened, burned-out shell.

Reconstruction took three years. During the remainder of the Madison Administration, the couple lived in rented houses, where the incomparable Dolley held court, and the President conducted executive

Admiring guests inspect the "exceedingly fine" presents sent to Nellie Grant on her marriage to Algernon Charles Frederick Sartoris in May 1874. Frank Leslie's Illustrated Newspaper lists a "dessert set of eighty-four silver pieces," a "very handsome silver ice-cream service," and a lace handkerchief "such as sell for $500."

affairs in an atmosphere of renewed confidence following the country's second confrontation with the British.

When James Monroe and his family moved into the rebuilt White House in the fall of 1817, its exterior had been painted a gleaming white. Handsomely restored inside, it contained elegantly carved and gilded furniture and decorative objects, much of it ordered by Monroe from France. Nor were the appearances deceptive. The new facade and furnishings marked a return to the pomp and protocol of earlier days.

Guests at the first New Year's reception had a preview of the changed rules when foreign diplomats were greeted with elaborate protocol before the public was admitted. From then on, Monroe insisted, as had Washington and Adams, that respect be shown the United States by placing foreign ministers "upon much the same footing . . . of form and ceremony" as that required of American ministers at European courts. This meant that diplomats would come to the White House only by invitation, or after requesting a formal audience with the President.

First Lady Elizabeth Monroe adopted a chillier social tone. She refused to continue the exhausting custom of making first calls, or even returning them. Eliza Hay, the Monroes' married daughter who lived in the White House with her husband, carried on her own feud with diplomatic-corps wives over the etiquette of paying calls.

THE DRASTIC CHANGE from the Madisons' warmth and accessibility alienated Washington's social leaders. They retaliated by boycotting the Monroes' "at homes."

"The drawing-room of the President was opened last night to a 'beggarly row of empty chairs,' " wrote Mrs. William Winston Seaton, wife of a prominent Washington newspaper editor. "Only five females attended, three of whom were foreigners."

More steam came from the teapot tempest when plans were announced for the wedding of pretty little Maria Monroe, not yet 17, to her cousin and her father's secretary, Samuel Laurence Gouverneur. The first White House marriage of a President's daughter would be private, the family decreed. Foreign diplomats were pointedly advised "to take no notice" of the event.

Afterward Mrs. Seaton commented briefly, "The New York style was adopted. . . . Only the attendants, the relations, and a few old friends of the bride and groom witnessed the ceremony. . . ."

In long-range social prestige, however, the White House always wins. Washington society eventually accepted the Monroes' rules of etiquette, along with their hospitality. Moreover, future First Ladies would be forever indebted to Elizabeth Monroe for freeing them from the demands of local sociabilities.

The Monroes' successors, John Quincy Adams and his wife, continued the high style of entertaining, bringing to it a background of the longest and most varied diplomatic and social experience abroad that any President has ever had. John Quincy, son of the first President to

FRANK LESLIE'S
ILLUSTRATED
NEWSPAPER

Entered according to Act of Congress, in the year 1886, by Mrs. Frank Leslie, in the Office of the Librarian of Congress at Washington.—Entered at the Post Office, New York, N. Y., as Second-class Matter.

No. 1,603.—Vol. LXII.]   NEW YORK—FOR THE WEEK ENDING JUNE 12, 1886.   [Price, 10 Cents. $4.00 Yearly. 13 Weeks, $1.00.

WASHINGTON, D. C.—THE WEDDING AT THE WHITE HOUSE, JUNE 2ND—THE MOTHER'S KISS.

FROM A SKETCH BY C. BUNNELL.—SEE PAGE 261.

live in the White House, had served in United States missions at many courts, including Prussia, the Netherlands, and England. His wife, Louisa Johnson Adams, born in London to an American father and an English mother, was a brilliant scholar and an accomplished hostess. Well read in Greek, French, and English literature, she wrote verse in French, played the harp and spinet, and maintained her equanimity under the heavy pressure of official entertaining.

"This evening was the sixth drawing-room," President Adams wrote in his diary after one of the public levees that were held every fortnight. "Very much crowded; sixteen Senators, perhaps sixty members of the House of Representatives, and multitudes of strangers . . . these parties are becoming more and more insupportable. . . ."

As a conscientious New Englander, however, Adams never shirked his duty. He met punctiliously with his guests and served even more elaborate refreshments than had his predecessor. The loaded trays carried by waiters threading their way through crowded state rooms held ice cream, coffee, tea, cakes, jellies, wines, and liqueurs—plus various imported West Indies fruits in season.

Perhaps the most notable dinner presided over by John Quincy Adams was one in 1825 honoring the Marquis de Lafayette on his 68th birthday. The French hero of the Revolutionary War, who was paying a return visit to America, responded thus to the President's toasts to his and George Washington's birthdays: "To the Fourth of July," he said, "the birthday of liberty in both continents."

The Adams family also held a historic wedding. On February 25, 1828, young John Adams, grandson of one President and son of another, married his cousin Mary Catherine Hellen, who had lived with the family in the White House. The event marks the only time that a President's son has been wed in the mansion. The ceremony was held in the first-floor oval room—now the Blue Room—which was decorated then in crimson and gold.

It was not an altogether happy occasion for the Adams family. The President had disapproved of the match, probably because fickle Mary Catherine had flirted earlier with John's two brothers. But the reception provided a bright note to an otherwise gloomy election year. Even the reserved and formal President unbent enough to dance the Virginia reel.

John Quincy Adams ended his one-term Presidency in deep chagrin over his defeat by the West's magnetic general, Andrew Jackson. He

Grover Cleveland, the only President married in the White House, accepts congratulations while his bride, Frances Folsom, kisses her mother. Rice and old slippers (above) rain down as the Clevelands leave on their honeymoon.

did not linger to attend the inaugural ceremonies, which culminated in the most boisterous celebration ever seen at the White House.

The enthusiastic followers of the veteran Indian fighter and hero of the Battle of New Orleans poured into Washington from far and near to see the "People's President" installed in the highest post of the land. Frontiersmen, clerks, and bankers, some with wives and children, jammed the boardinghouses and hotels, slept in the streets, and whooped it up in the bars. "It was like the inundation of the northern barbarians into Rome. . . ," said one eyewitness.

After applauding Jackson's inaugural address at the Capitol, the crowd moved on to enjoy the White House reception—to the accompaniment of crashing china and glassware. Attendants lured many of the unruly guests out to the lawn for punch served from buckets.

Inside, merrymakers stood in muddy boots on satin chairs to catch a glimpse of their new leader, while would-be handshakers backed him against the wall. The President escaped the mob's further embrace only by slipping out and spending the night at the "Wigwam," as Capital residents had nicknamed the nearby Gadsby's Hotel.

YET THE RUDE OPENING of the Jackson Administration was far from an accurate foretaste of "Old Hickory's" tenure in the White House. Accustomed to the fine surroundings of his Tennessee plantation, the President immediately sought appropriations from Congress to improve the mansion, which the legislators had allowed to fall into a shabby state during the Adams Administration.

Throughout Jackson's two terms, a willing Congress provided him with nearly $50,000 to refurbish the house and to build the massive, rectangular North Portico to complement the gracefully curving south entrance added by Monroe.

Before the end of Jackson's first year, the great East Room was at last completely and handsomely furnished to permit the ceremonial use for which it was originally planned. The President was particularly interested in having the Monroe chairs repaired and reupholstered, according to one account, so that people would not be kept "standing upon their legs as they do before kings and emperors."

At his official receptions and suppers, Jackson also offered guests sumptuous repasts, including the best wines and liqueurs, and every kind of meat and fowl the lush new land afforded.

But Jackson himself had little interest in either food or drink. Even his victory at the polls was an empty one, for he had come to the White House in deep grief—and cold fury. His beloved wife, Rachel, had died of a heart attack shortly after his election, and he believed her death was caused by malicious campaign gossip that stirred up an old scandal about their marriage. They had wed 30 years earlier in the mistaken belief that her first husband had obtained a divorce. After the divorce was granted, the Jacksons remarried, but political enemies never stopped blackening her name.

The President was thus disposed to defend the reputation of another woman he felt to be similarly maligned. A "petticoat war" erupted when wives of high government officials refused to receive pretty Peggy O'Neale Eaton, daughter of an innkeeper and wife of Jackson's Secretary of War, John Eaton. Though Jackson pressured their husbands, the wives still would not recognize the woman they accused of accepting Eaton's attentions before her first husband died. All but one of Jackson's Cabinet Members resigned before the problem was resolved by the appointment of Eaton first as governor of Florida and then in 1836 as United States minister to Spain.

The last open house held by Jackson was almost as rowdy as his first. On the eve of leaving office in 1837, he was presented with a 1,400-pound cheese. Placing the huge gift in the north hall, he invited the public to come and eat as much as they liked in celebration of George Washington's birthday.

The people came in droves. What they didn't eat dropped on the floor and was trod into the carpets; the smell lingered for weeks. And the whole affair, some said, effectively discouraged public entertaining by incoming President Martin Van Buren, who was Jackson's Vice President and his handpicked choice for the nation's top office.

Whatever his reason, Van Buren—a widower for 18 years—discontinued all public receptions except those on New Year's Day and July 4. Instead of the openhanded hospitality of the Jackson era, he arranged small, exclusive dinner parties, where both friendly and opposing political leaders traded lively repartee.

The President's four bachelor sons, who lived with him and shared his social and political interests, presented an irresistible challenge to Washington matchmakers. Dolley Madison, who was by now an aging but still romantic widow, won the prize by introducing Van Buren's eldest son, Abraham, to Angelica Singleton, a lovely young relative of hers then visiting the Capital from South Carolina.

FRANK LESLIE'S ILLUSTRATED NEWSPAPER, FEBRUARY 21, 1885, TINTED BY P. HALL BAGLIE

Cartoon satirizes curious rural visitors to the White House after its 1882 redecoration by President Chester A. Arthur.

As Mrs. Abraham Van Buren, charming Angelica made a perfect hostess for her father-in-law. But the President's enemies found a rich lode of political capital in what they pictured as selfish high living in the Executive Mansion while the country suffered from a severe depression. Congressman Charles Ogle of Pennsylvania led the attack in blocking an appropriation of $3,665 for the mansion's maintenance.

In what would become famous as the "Gold Spoon Speech," he described Van Buren as one who used "knives, forks, and spoons of gold, that he may dine in the style of the monarchs of Europe." He spent "the People's cash in . . . green finger cups, in which to wash his pretty tapering, soft, white lily fingers," and ate fancy French foods instead of good American " 'hog and hominy,' 'fried meat and gravy' . . . with a mug of 'hard cider.' "

Van Buren's defenders assembled figures to prove that their man actually was costing the taxpayers less for house expenses than had any other President. But the gold-spoon image had been created, and in 1840 the voters elected the President's opponent, William Henry Harrison, candidate of the Whig "Log Cabin and Hard Cider" Party.

The next shift in administrations came with a suddenness no one could have anticipated. Former General Harrison, hero of a famous Indian battle on the Tippecanoe River, was at 68 the oldest man to become President up to that time. He rode horseback to the Capitol and in an icy wind delivered the longest inaugural speech in history. Other exposures to wintry weather followed, leading to a cold that turned into pneumonia. One month after his inauguration, he was dead.

Harrison's wife, Anna, was the only First Lady who never acted in her official role. She did not even see the White House. At the time of the inauguration she was unable to stand the rough coach-and-steamer trip from her home on the Ohio frontier. She was about to leave when a messenger rode up with news of the President's death. It was too late to attend the state funeral for her husband—the first President to die in office. She remained in Ohio, where Harrison had made his career—and where their grandson, Benjamin Harrison, would start on his path to the Presidency nearly half a century later.

Thus the White House received an unexpected master in John Tyler, who as the Vice Presidential candidate had been the last half of Harrison's catchy campaign slogan, "Tippecanoe and Tyler Too."

P RESIDENT TYLER, labeled "His Accidency" by unkind critics, was destined to remain in the mansion only a single term. But he brought to it in turn two wives as different as they could be. Gentle Letitia, his first wife and mother of eight children, led the retiring life of an invalid until her death in 1842. Acting in her stead, her daughter-in-law, Priscilla (Mrs. Robert Tyler), performed as a highly successful official hostess on such glittering occasions as the state dinner and ball given for the Prince de Joinville, son of Louis Philippe of France.

Letitia Tyler appeared in company only once in the White House, at the wedding of her daughter Elizabeth to William Waller of Virginia. Wearing a simple gown and a soft lace cap that framed her still-handsome dark eyes, she sat quietly during the festivities.

"Lizzie has had quite a grand wedding," Mrs. Robert Tyler wrote of the event, which all Washington society attended. Dolley Madison, now 73 and popular as ever, was there, as well as the eloquent Daniel Webster, Tyler's Secretary of State and a great friend of the family.

In his deep, resonant voice, Webster quoted Sir Walter Scott when

"Princess Alice," on the arm of her father, President Theodore Roosevelt, descends the grand stairway for her 1906 marriage to Congressman Nicholas Longworth. "It wasn't like that at all," Mrs. Longworth said in later years of the newspaper illustration. "We came down in the elevator in the back and walked down the hall to the East Room."

someone remarked that the President's pretty daughter was giving up Capital "belleship" to live in quiet Williamsburg.

"Love rules the court, the camp, the grove. . . ," he said—and spoke more prophetically than he knew. For in June 1844, eight months before the end of his term, the widower President took a second wife in a private ceremony in New York City.

The bride, lighthearted 24-year-old Julia Gardiner—a belle at home and abroad before her marriage—frankly enjoyed the attention she received as the nation's First Lady.

Seated in a large armchair on a platform in the Blue Room, the erstwhile "Rose of Long Island" greeted guests with the air of a queen. In a white satin ball gown and gleaming headdress adorned with diamonds and ostrich feathers, she led the dancing in the East Room as gentlemen whirled their partners in the then-daring waltz. At one reception she introduced a bouncy Bohemian dance called the polka and started it toward wide popularity.

After an especially triumphant evening, Julia Tyler wrote her mother with girlish delight, "the British Minister, Pakenham, was there . . . and devoted to me. At least fifty members of Congress paid their respects to me, and all at one time."

To pleasure-loving members of the Capital's higher echelons, the dancing steps of the second Mrs. Tyler gave way far too quickly to the dogged tread of all-work-and-no-play President Polk, and his handsome but straitlaced Sarah. New rules permitted no dancing, card-playing, or similar diversions. The proper Polks did their duty, offering the required number of formal dinners and grand receptions, but no food or beverages refreshed the great dry public gatherings.

A guest who ventured to compliment the First Lady on the "genteel assemblage" at one of these receptions met Sarah Polk's dignified reply: "Sir, I have never seen it otherwise."

The next three Presidents—Zachary Taylor, Millard Fillmore, and Franklin Pierce—had little chance to enliven the Washington social scene. The popular former general, "Old Rough and Ready" Taylor, died after only 16 months in office. During that time his delicate wife, Margaret, had relied on their married daughter, Betty Bliss, to do the honors at official functions.

Ailing Abigail Fillmore also was forced to delegate many of her hostess chores to her daughter, Mary Abigail. Yet, as the President's wife, she managed to put in an appearance and to greet guests at a surprising number of dinners and receptions in spite of delicate health

To the Emperor and people of Germany and to Prince Henry of Prussia! Offering a toast, Theodore Roosevelt turns toward his guest of honor. At his left stands Sir Julian Pauncefote, the British Ambassador. Protocol had fretted the President—"Will the Prince take Mrs. Roosevelt [to dinner] while I walk in solemn state by myself? How do we do it anyhow?" His solution: a reception with ladies, followed by a stag dinner served in the East Room. Flags and eagles of the two countries brighten the menu for the Kaiser's brother.

and the pain that came from standing on a permanently injured ankle.

One of the gloomiest periods in White House entertaining prevailed during the Pierce Administration, which began soon after the Pierces had seen their last surviving child, Benjamin, killed in a railroad accident. Naturally limited at first, White House social functions continued thereafter in a stiff and somber atmosphere, which extended even to Mrs. Pierce's large table bouquets of rigidly wired japonicas.

The return of what a reporter called "joy and gladness in the Executive Mansion" came, ironically enough, in the ominous pre-Civil War term of President James Buchanan. One cause for joy was Buchanan's beautiful young niece and ward, Harriet Lane. As his official hostess, she presided over so many brilliant balls and sumptuous banquets that the White House was compared to a European court; and it frequently drew titled travelers.

Journalists also wrote about the first diplomatic mission to Washington from Imperial Japan in the spring of 1860. Delivering a commercial treaty, the 60-member entourage created a sensation in the mansion's East Room, where curious Americans climbed on chairs to view the envoys' Oriental dress and exotic hairstyles.

As a final social coup in his politically weak administration, President Buchanan welcomed the Prince of Wales, later Britain's Edward VII, as a houseguest. Miss Lane arranged a state dinner with royal protocol, followed by fireworks on the lawn. But the public reception for the prince turned into a roughhouse.

"The Royal party have certainly seen Democracy unshackled for once," wrote a New York correspondent. "The rush . . . was terrible. People clambered in and jumped out of the windows. . . ."

DURING THE CIVIL WAR, White House entertaining took a new direction. The Union Capital was crowded with Northern Army and Navy officers, war contractors, and assorted visitors who came to see President Lincoln and to share the First Family's hospitality. Special dinners and receptions were given for high government officials, staff officers, and diplomats.

To the President's weekly public levees came motley crowds of soldiers and day laborers along with the most fashionable ladies and gentlemen. Attired "with gloves and without gloves; clean and dirty. . . ," they all pressed toward "the tall, rapidly bobbing head of the good 'Abe,' as he shook hands with his guests," recalled one bystander; and "when anyone he knew came along, he bent himself down to the necessary level, and seemed to whisper a few words in the ear, in pleasant, homely fashion."

Mary Lincoln held afternoon receptions, too, and carefully planned major social events. But nothing she did could please her relentless critics. If she served fine food, the First Lady was wasting money while brave boys died at the front. If she held only a reception instead of a formal dinner, her critics said she must be saving money for the personal finery that everyone knew to be her weakness. Yet the same carping public committed shocking acts of vandalism in the President's home. Guests at Lincoln's second inaugural reception cut souvenirs of floral designs from brocaded window draperies and lace curtains; damage in general was extensive.

After Lincoln's assassination, ruthless collectors ravaged the house. "Silver and dining ware were carried off . . . ," wrote an eyewitness. "It was plundered not only of ornaments but of heavy articles of furniture. Costly sofas and chairs were cut and injured."

Following the Civil War, White House hospitality continued to reflect the attitudes of each new set of residents as they adapted themselves and their house to changing times.

When Andrew Johnson and his family moved into the shabby building in the summer of 1865, they brought to its renovation a sturdy common sense that might well have served as an example to politicians during the turbulent days of Reconstruction.

"We are plain people from the mountains of Tennessee," said the Johnsons' older daughter, Martha Patterson, who directed most of the work and took over as official hostess for her invalid mother. "I trust too much will not be expected of us," she added, and then proceeded to extend the family's hospitality with natural good taste and a charm that surprised and won over Washington sophisticates.

The Johnsons also showed how "plain people" could stand with dignity during the terrible weeks before the President's impeachment trial ended in his vindication. But it was a miserable time for all.

The inauguration of popular Union general Ulysses S. Grant on March 4, 1869, finally opened the floodgates for long-deferred Capital celebrations. Mrs. Grant relished her role as mistress of the White House. She found it, she wrote, "a garden spot of orchids . . . a constant feast of cleverness and wit, with men who were the brainiest . . . and women unrivalled for beauty, talent and tact."

William Howard Taft receives socialites on the south lawn.

The Grants entertained often and lavishly. In 1874 King David Kalakaua of the Sandwich Islands—now Hawaii—became the first ruling monarch to visit the White House. At a state dinner in his honor, three of the King's retinue stood behind him, and one examined each dish before his master accepted it.

The peak of the Grants' social activity came when their idolized daughter, Ellen (Nellie), wed a young Englishman, Algernon Charles Frederick Sartoris, whom she had met on a trip abroad. The 18-year-old bride, dressed in white satin trimmed with yards of Brussels round-point lace, was married amid elaborate floral decorations in the great East Room. The wedding breakfast included an awesome assortment of elegant dishes for the most fashionable social event of the season. But one participant at the feast was plainly unhappy. Tears filled the eyes of President Grant, who was losing his only daughter.

If the Grant Administration typified mid-Victorian style in heavy food and intricate decor, President and Mrs. Rutherford B. Hayes followed as perfect examples of the era's ideal of moral rectitude.

Few White House scenes were ever more sedate than the Sunday-evening hymn sings and prayers that Congressional and Cabinet friends shared with the Presidential family. No alcoholic beverage was served at any function—a prohibition that earned Mrs. Hayes the nickname of "Lemonade Lucy" and brought a quip from one guest that "water flowed like wine."

The more relaxed yet intellectual social atmosphere that marked the beginning of James A. Garfield's term as the next President is often obscured by the tragedy of his assassination. Both he and his wife, Lucretia, were warm, cultured people. A classical scholar, Garfield sometimes performed the trick of simultaneously writing Greek with one hand and Latin with the other. Mrs. Garfield was perhaps the first First Lady to initiate serious research on White House history.

Then, without warning, the bright six-month tenure of the Garfields ended on July 2, 1881, with shots fired by a demented office seeker. When the new Chief Executive, former Vice President Chester A. Arthur, took over, he began making some of the most drastic changes yet seen in the appearance of the mansion.

"I will not live in a house like this," he said after inspecting the accumulation of mixed and battered furniture and ornaments. Nor did he. Arthur sold at public auction 24 wagonloads of discards, lavishly redecorated the mansion, and installed the famous Tiffany glass screen on the formal first floor.

A rich widower, President Arthur became the most eligible catch in town. His huge wardrobe and swanky carriage were topics of conversation, his elegant dinners the most sought after. But he remained an elusive prospect and left as he came, a widower.

The people's next choice was America's second bachelor President, Grover Cleveland, who soon placed himself beyond the reach of contriving matchmakers by choosing his own bride.

THE WEDDING OF THE ONLY PRESIDENT TO MARRY in the White House created a furor in 1886, when 49-year-old Cleveland took as his wife lovely 21-year-old Frances Folsom, daughter of his former law partner. The couple planned a private wedding; the bridegroom issued fewer than 40 handwritten invitations to close friends and relatives. But Cleveland had the mansion turned into a bower of flowers for the occasion, and church bells all over the city announced the end of the ceremony as a 21-gun salute boomed from the Navy Yard.

As a hostess, Frances Cleveland proved as capable as she was beautiful. She organized functions well in advance and showed her stamina

President and Mrs. Dwight D. Eisenhower greet Queen Elizabeth II and Prince Philip of Great Britain on their arrival at the North Portico. Of his royal guests' hectic, historic, and cordial four-day stay at the White House in October 1957, Eisenhower recalled, "This was one ceremonial visit that we were sorry to see end."

Grace and glitter in the glare of photographers' lights: With President and Mrs. John F. Kennedy, Shah Mohammad Reza Pahlavi of Iran and his Empress Farah enter the White House for a state dinner during their visit in April 1962. Below, the Kennedys and their guests applaud renowned cellist Pablo Casals after his East Room concert in 1961.

by shaking hands with an estimated 9,000 guests at one public reception. She arranged at-home days so that all women who wished to meet her could. Indeed, energetic Mrs. Cleveland so enjoyed life in the White House that she left tearfully in 1889, remarking to a member of the house staff that she and her husband would be back.

Four years later she kept her promise. Cleveland was reelected and became the only President to serve nonconsecutive terms.

The Victorian Age gave us two more First Ladies, each representative of the period in her own way. Caroline Scott Harrison, wife of Benjamin Harrison, brought to her new role the same energy she had shown in church and club work back in Ohio. A model of domesticity, she presided over the White House with genteel efficiency.

President William McKinley's wife, Ida, embodied a no less typically Victorian image of the delicate female. Though in poor health, she made valiant efforts to cope with official schedules. She attended exhausting state dinners, at which the usual seating arrangement was changed to place her beside her devoted husband, who could thus see to her needs. From a chair near the receiving line at receptions, Ida greeted guests but held a bouquet to foil handshakers.

As the 20th century arrived, it was no coincidence that the dynamic character and deeds of Theodore Roosevelt reflected America's exuberance, growing power, and influence.

By moving his offices to the new West Wing and remodeling the mansion's state rooms after the simple elegance of the early Federal period, the President at once gained quarters for increasing executive business and created a more appropriate setting for the nation's official entertaining. From December 1902, when the renovation was completed, social functions began to take on the more regulated character of modern times. The Roosevelts employed the first White House social secretary, and the President delegated a government official to untangle sticky problems of precedence involving diplomatic and political rivalries.

Roosevelt imparted his own ebullience to every White House event—from a reunion with the Rough Riders of the Spanish-American War to a Japanese jujitsu exhibition in the East Room.

T. R.'s charming wife, Edith, brought to her official duties a poise that led the President's military aide, Archie Butt, to write that she spent seven years as First Lady "without ever having made a mistake." But it was Roosevelt's eldest daughter, Alice—by his first wife, who had died shortly after childbirth—who set off the social fireworks of the administration. "Princess Alice," as the newspapers called her, became the most headlined debutante and bride of her generation.

A thousand guests came to the White House wedding and reception when she married Congressman Nicholas Longworth of Ohio. Her gifts

Dancers of the Harkness House for Ballet Arts perform the premiere of "Classical Symphony" at the dedication of a new portable stage, designed to match the decor of the East Room and given to the White House in September 1965. ▷

Japanese guests in silk kimonos and obis chat with Mrs. Johnson in the State Dining Room. This 1965 reception followed ceremonies at the Tidal Basin, where the First Lady planted two flowering cherry trees—part of a gift of 3,800 saplings from Japan. Mrs. William Howard Taft planted the first cherry tree beside the Tidal Basin in 1912.

included rare silks and jade sent by the Empress Dowager of China, a pearl necklace presented by the Cuban government, a feather duster, and a hogshead of popcorn.

The last eight decades of social history at the White House have clearly shown how life in the Executive Residence has been colored by each family's personality and background.

President and Mrs. William H. Taft gave a touch of the Orient to their quarters by introducing furnishings from the Philippines, where he had served as the first American civil governor. The Tafts were also first to entertain on the terraced roof of the new west extension, where they sat at wicker tables under Chinese lanterns.

Woodrow Wilson, who like John Tyler became a widower in office and who also brought a second wife to the mansion, had firm ideas of his role as host. Regardless of pressures, he refused to invite anyone to the White House to further even the most precious of his programs. "I will not permit my home to be used for political purposes," he declared. And, although he presided with good humor at official parties, he preferred small dinners in the Jeffersonian manner—animated by witty and intellectual conversation.

President Wilson and his first wife, Ellen, launched two of their daughters into marriage at the White House. The wedding of their sec-

British Prime Minister Harold Wilson, seated to the right of President Johnson, leans forward to hear Secretary of State Dean Rusk report on world affairs in 1965. British and American officials conferred on mutual problems at the working luncheon. The wallpaper in the President's Dining Room portrays a less friendly period between the two countries—the Revolutionary War.

ond daughter, Jessie, to law professor Francis B. Sayre was the outstanding social event of the administration, though perhaps not so grandiose as one headline writer put it: "NATIONS OF ALL THE WORLD DO HOMAGE TO WHITE HOUSE BRIDE AS SHE TAKES SOLEMN VOWS AMID SCENES OF UNEQUALED SPLENDOR." Six months afterward, the Wilsons' youngest daughter, Eleanor, married Secretary of the Treasury William Gibbs McAdoo with little display because of her mother's failing health.

After the grim days of World War I, and the gloom of Wilson's long illness, brought on by the strain of his lost campaign for the League of Nations, the arrival of genial Warren G. Harding seemed to bring back the pleasant days of "normalcy" he had promised.

Not only did the new President and his wife, Florence, reopen the doors for large and frequent official gatherings, but they also dined almost daily with Harding's card-playing cronies and other close friends. They welcomed the public for tours of the mansion, and on such occasions, Mrs. Harding sometimes appeared unexpectedly and shook hands with astonished, delighted sightseers.

Then, suddenly, following the President's heart attack and death during a trip to the West in 1923, the convivial period ended. To the Executive Mansion came the rock-ribbed New Englander and former Vice President, Calvin Coolidge, and his charming wife, Grace.

Social life during the Coolidge Administration was notable for the many anecdotes it produced concerning the granite reserve and wry humor of the President. The early-morning breakfasts to which Coolidge invited Members of Congress—often to the dismay of late sleepers—gave Capital raconteurs some of their best stories. One told of the time the President poured coffee and cream into his saucer. As a few guests followed suit, Coolidge calmly put the saucer on the floor for his dog.

The most famous guest of the time, loquacious Queen Marie of Romania, was entertained at a state dinner in 1926. According to Chief Usher Ike Hoover, the queen made strenuous efforts to get "Silent Cal" to talk, but "was not any more successful than others who had tried it before." The whole affair was odd, the Chief Usher noted, for the visit, including ceremonial greetings, the meal, and farewells, took only an hour and forty-five minutes.

Yet, in the matter of etiquette, President Coolidge inaugurated what has become an indispensable aid in conducting state visits. Following an awkward incident in which wartime enemies were seated together at an official dinner, he established a Protocol Office in the State Department to handle procedures for such visits. Today its chief has a staff of more than 70 people to arrange programs, determine precedence, and plan menus to fit the specific needs of each delegation.

White House entertaining reached new heights when President Herbert Hoover assumed office amid a seemingly endless boom economy. Even after America's Great Depression struck in the autumn of 1929, the wealthy President and his wife, Lou, continued to invite a record number of guests for breakfast, lunch, and dinner, though they personally met the expenses not only for their private parties but also for many of the official ones.

No one could assume, however, that such hospitality marked indifference to the nation's problems. The Quaker President had long shown his humanity in war and postwar relief work in food distribution, and no President ever worked harder than Hoover as he labored to solve the country's gargantuan economic troubles. At times he would gulp his meals so fast, a member of the domestic staff recalled, that "the servants made bets on how long it would take . . . 'Nine minutes, fifteen seconds,' or whatever. . . ."

FRANKLIN DELANO ROOSEVELT and his big, gregarious clan came next, to meet the challenge of the Depression and usher in the longest, most varied social period yet.

Guests pouring into and out of the mansion between March 1933 and April 1945 included students, poets, playwrights, labor leaders, nuclear scientists, prime ministers, and presidents. British Prime Minister Winston Churchill came often, and the mysterious visitor of 1942, known only as Mr. Brown, turned out to be Soviet Foreign Minister V. M. Molotov on a World War II mission to speed up the opening of an Allied second front in Europe.

Following their wedding in the East Room in 1967, Lynda Johnson Robb and Charles Robb (below) walk under swords held by six of the bridegroom's Marine comrades. On the arm of her father, Tricia Nixon (above) enters the Rose Garden in 1971 for the first outdoor wedding in White House history. After the ceremony, Mr. and Mrs. Edward Finch Cox return to the mansion for a reception.

The war gave a regal dimension to the Roosevelts' hospitality with the appearance of royal refugees fleeing Nazi occupation in Europe. Some, like the Crown Prince and Princess of Norway and Queen Wilhelmina of the Netherlands, became temporary houseguests. Others, like the Kings of Greece and Yugoslavia, were briefly feted.

Older Washingtonians recall the White House visit of Britain's King George VI and Queen Elizabeth just before war erupted in 1939. Down the hall from the family rooms on the second floor, the King occupied the Lincoln suite, his Queen, the Rose suite, later called the Queens' Bedroom. Screens separated the royal and Presidential quarters.

Thus each administration has left its social imprint here since John and Abigail Adams first welcomed leaders of official Washington to their formal "levees."

By the time of President Harry S. Truman and his wife, Bess, the "season" had expanded to include half a dozen state dinners and as many Congressional and other large receptions. Some were so well attended that guests stood almost shoulder to shoulder.

At a reception in 1948, the chandelier in the Blue Room tinkled a warning that the structure was in critically shaky condition. Then for four years, while the White House underwent reconstruction, the Tru-

mans lived across the street in the government's guest residence, Blair House. In 1951 Britain's young Princess Elizabeth and her husband, Philip, Duke of Edinburgh, spent several days there with the Trumans.

The following year, the Presidential family moved back into the restored Executive Mansion just in time to welcome as houseguests Queen Juliana of the Netherlands and her consort, Prince Bernhard.

But Capital life was changing in the postwar era. State visitors came so frequently from newly independent nations and as a result of foreign-policy conferences and fast modern transport that the White House could no longer accommodate them.

Since the latter part of the Eisenhower Administration, most official guests have stayed at Blair House during their state visits. In fact, only once during Eisenhower's second term did such guests sleep in the mansion. Elizabeth II, Queen of Great Britain, and Prince Philip occupied the Rose and Lincoln suites, as had her mother and father nearly 20 years before.

Under the lively direction of John F. and Jacqueline Kennedy in the early 1960's, official entertaining changed further. President Kennedy banished receiving lines whenever possible and chatted informally with guests in the connecting state rooms. Shorter, simpler dinners allowed

NATIONAL GEOGRAPHIC PHOTOGRAPHER JOSEPH H. BAILEY (BOTH)

President Ford stands to toast Queen Elizabeth II of Great Britain at a Bicentennial dinner in her honor on July 7, 1976. Lilies and greenery decorate the pavilion erected in the Rose Garden for the occasion. After dinner (above), Mrs. Ford dances with Prince Philip in the State Dining Room.

NATIONAL GEOGRAPHIC PHOTOGRAPHER JOSEPH H. BAILEY; DONALD J. CRUMP, NATIONAL GEOGRAPHIC STAFF (RIGHT)

guests more time to dance and to watch performances of famous musicians, ballet dancers, opera singers, and actors.

Then came the crack of rifle shots in Dallas—and a black interlude of international mourning for the bright, lost promise of a murdered President. When social life returned to the White House, the new host brought with him a quarter century of Capital friendships and service, first as Representative and Senator from Texas, then as Vice President. It was not surprising that an atmosphere of Texas Americana pervaded the private and official parties of Lyndon B. Johnson and his wife, Claudia, better known by her childhood nickname, "Lady Bird."

Informal cordiality also warmed two of the most publicized social events ever held in Washington—the weddings of the Johnson daugh-

Trees ablaze with tiny lights offer a glittery backdrop for the barbecue given by President and Mrs. Jimmy Carter on the west terrace during the visit of the Japanese prime minister in May 1979. Like the Tafts, who were the first to hold dinners on the rooftop terrace, the Carters frequently entertained outdoors. In June 1978 a jazz festival on the south lawn featured Eubie Blake, pounding out ragtime with a gusto that denied his 95 years (below).

ters, Luci and Lynda. The news coverage demonstrated the public's avid interest in every detail of a First Family's life.

Scores of reporters, photographers, and television crews recorded Luci's August 1966 church wedding to Patrick J. Nugent, of Illinois, and the reception at the flower-adorned mansion. When Lynda married Capt. Charles S. Robb of the U. S. Marine Corps, sixteen months later, both ceremony and reception took place in the White House. There, telephones, typewriters, and closed-circuit television were provided for some 500 attending members of the news media.

In January 1969 the spotlight on executive entertaining moved from the Johnsons to the Nixons, another family with two daughters. But the resemblance ended there, for President and Mrs. Nixon, like those who

The East Room offers a display case for the performing arts. The Alvin Ailey dancers entertain Carter guests in 1978 (left). In 1981, noted soprano Beverly Sills listens as 18-year-old violinist Ida Levin plays a duet with her sponsor, veteran piano-virtuoso Rudolf Serkin (right).

went before, soon produced an entertainment pattern all their own that included programs ranging from rock concerts to comedy routines to Shakespearean drama. One innovation was a series of Sunday-morning services attended by associates and friends of the family. Held in the East Room and presided over by leaders of various faiths, the services were followed by a social hour and refreshments served in the State Dining Room.

But nothing attracts more attention than a wedding. The Nixons' younger daughter, Julie, missed most of the fanfare by marrying David Eisenhower, grandson of the former President, in New York City, shortly before her father was inaugurated.

Her sister, Tricia, however, chose the White House for her marriage to law student Edward Finch Cox of New York. She arranged for the ceremony to be performed in the famous Rose Garden. Thus, on June 12, 1971, she became the first President's daughter to have an outdoor wedding at the Executive Mansion.

Some 400 guests were seated in the garden, which resembled an old-fashioned valentine decorated with masses of roses, lilies, and petunias. Standing before the altar, in an open, wrought-iron pavilion laced with white blossoms, the President gave the bride away. Afterward, blonde, diminutive Tricia, wearing a lacy Juliet cap, cascading veil, and white organdy dress, walked back to the mansion with her tall, smiling bridegroom—to open the reception and dancing that followed.

Tricia's wedding marked the social high point of her family's tenure. As events unfolded over the next three years, the Nixon Administration ended in political scandals and the President's resignation, and with a new family in the old house.

From August 1974 to January 1977 the Gerald Fords made their own

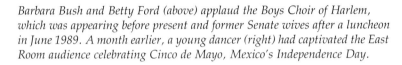

*Barbara Bush and Betty Ford (above) applaud the Boys Choir of Harlem,
which was appearing before present and former Senate wives after a luncheon
in June 1989. A month earlier, a young dancer (right) had captivated the East
Room audience celebrating Cinco de Mayo, Mexico's Independence Day.*

brand of White House history. Among happier events on the social
side, guests may remember lively musical and theatrical programs
capped by dancing in the big Entrance Hall. There Betty Ford, who once
studied modern dance with the noted Martha Graham Dance Company
of New York, whirled gracefully with the President and other partners.

With the Georgia Carters, still another regional design went into the
tapestry of White House hospitality, which never ceases to repeat the
infinite variety of American life.

"Natural," "spontaneous," and "family oriented" became words often
used by the media to describe the Carters' southern style. Yet, if some
found elements of close-knit, small-town entertaining at Jimmy and
Rosalynn Carter's receptions and dinners, there is no doubt that the
top-notch American and European performers they introduced on the
East Room stage rivaled the list of world-famous musicians, ballet dancers, and opera stars who enchanted audiences during the Kennedy
Administration.

Still, the more it changes, the more hospitality retains its symbolic
meaning in the house that belongs to all Americans. And never more so
than when a President and his wife receive visiting dignitaries representing a cross section of global power and influence.

Where else could you find dinner guests who included 18 heads of
Latin American states, 25 U. S. Senators, a former President, Gerald
Ford, and a former First Lady, Lady Bird Johnson? This spectacular
event occurred during the Carter Administration in September 1977, after the ceremonial signing of the treaties to transfer the Panama Canal to
the Republic of Panama.

Behind the glitter and ceremony of such state affairs, elaborate planning goes into making sure each is tailored to fit the national culture and

individual tastes of the guests of honor. To assure the success of the meal, the Reagans even tried out the complete dinner, down to the last detail, a week or ten days before the event.

For Italy's prime minister, Giulio Andreotti, the Bushes' guest list included Senators Alfonse D'Amato of New York and Pete Domenici of New Mexico; Lee Iacocca, chairman of Chrysler Corporation; and singer Frank Sinatra. At a dinner in honor of Polish Prime Minister Tadeusz Mazowiecki, Polish Americans were represented by Baseball Hall of Fame stars Stan Musial and Carl Yastrzemski, former National Security Adviser Zbigniew Brzezinski, Representative Dan Rostenkowski of Illinois, and Senator Frank Murkowski of Alabama.

The style of decorations and table settings for state dinners is classic and elegant; this reflects Mrs. Bush's own tastes. A longtime flower gardener, she frequently uses the set of china chosen by Lady Bird Johnson, which features the various state wildflowers in its borders. Menus are classic continental cuisine with personal touches by the Bushes. They often choose lobster from Maine, where they traditionally vacation, and select special desserts for distinguished guests. For a dinner

honoring Great Britain's Queen Elizabeth II, a very imaginative dessert was served at each table: marzipan cobblestones topped with a ten-inch dark-chocolate carriage filled with pistachio mousse and fresh raspberries.

The international flavor of these affairs is perhaps most apparent in the musical entertainment. During a dinner in honor of Prime Minister and Mrs. R.J.L. Hawke of Australia, the Army Strolling Strings serenaded them with "Waltzing Matilda," the unofficial national anthem of Australia. For Hungarian Prime Minister Jozsef Antall, pianist Van Cliburn performed music by Hungarian composer Franz Liszt.

Sometimes the visitors are treated to American music. President and Mrs. Carlos Andres Perez of Venezuela were entertained at a dinner by New Orleans jazz clarinetist Pete Fountain. At a dinner in honor of Lech Walesa, Poland's first elected President, Broadway and cabaret singer Karen Akers sang popular show tunes. For Soviet President and Mrs. Mikhail Gorbachev, American mezzo-soprano Frederica von Stade performed opera arias and selections from such American classics as *Porgy and Bess* and *Show Boat.*

A fife-and-drum corps parades on the south lawn (opposite, upper) during the arrival ceremony for Great Britain's Queen Elizabeth II and her consort, Prince Philip, on May 14, 1991. That night President and Mrs. Bush welcome the royal visitors on the North Portico (opposite, lower) for a state dinner in their honor. After dinner and a concert by diva Jessye Norman, the President and Vice President and their wives join dancers in the East Room (above).

3

THE FIRST FAMILY
AT HOME

IN SPITE OF ALL THE AIDS, comforts, and privileges that come to a President and his family, homemaking in a house that is also a national monument has its drawbacks.

When President Coolidge arrived at the White House in 1923, he tried to continue his pleasant after-dinner habit of sitting on his front porch—the great North Portico—and watching the people go by on Pennsylvania Avenue. So many pedestrians stopped to stare at him, however, that he gave up this modest form of relaxation.

It was President Coolidge, too, who once invited a Missouri Senator friend to accompany him on an evening walk outside the grounds. As they returned to the mansion, the Senator remarked facetiously, "I wonder who lives there."

"Nobody," replied the President. "They just come and go."

Coolidge's wry remark was only half true. Though Chief Executives have moved in and out with regularity, the White House has always been a place of extremely personal living. Indeed, the attention commanded by the Presidency intensifies and exaggerates the normal joys and sorrows of everyday family experience, the high moments of birth and death that are part of life here as in any other home.

Accentuated problems, too, face each First Lady in her highly visible role as the President's wife and as the mistress of a semipublic building.

In a quiet moment, Frances Cleveland catches up on her correspondence in the family quarters. Through the years, First Families have attempted, with varying success, to lead normal personal lives in the hectic White House.

FRANK LESLIE'S ILLUSTRATED NEWSPAPER, APRIL 3, 1880, LIBRARY OF CONGRESS, TINTED BY P. HALL BAGLIE

"Here we gather every evening," remarked President Hayes of his library, today's Yellow Oval Room. Family and friends listen while Carl Schurz, Secretary of the Interior, coaxes "fantasias and caprices" from the keys. On Sunday nights, Cabinet officers and Senators joined in singing hymns— "There is a land of pure delight," and "A few more years shall roll."

The public is keenly interested in, and often feels free to criticize, the way she runs her house, selects her dresses, or chooses to style her hair. Mrs. Hoover told of receiving a letter from an indignant tourist who complained about a mended curtain she had seen in one of the rooms. Eleanor Roosevelt remarked that she sometimes felt she was no longer clothing herself "but dressing a public monument."

The clothes and hairdos of a President's wife may sway fashions everywhere. Jacqueline Kennedy's fitted dresses, cloth coats, and bouffant hairstyle were copied around the world. When designers drastically lengthened skirts in 1970, many reporters asked Mrs. Nixon just how far from the floor she would wear her hems. About this time, French President Georges Pompidou, accompanied by his wife, arrived for a state visit—and Mrs. Pompidou's midi skirts received almost as much press coverage as did her husband's politics.

Betty Ford, who made her living as a model when she was a young woman studying dance, stayed in step with—and sometimes ahead of—current vogues. Some of Rosalynn Carter's outfits came from top American designers; but she showed her taste for simple dress by bringing her own sewing machine with her to the White House.

Nancy Reagan's preferences for elegant evening gowns and classic daytime suits were echoed wherever style-conscious women gathered. Following tradition, she donated her first inaugural ball gown to the Smithsonian Institution. "I feel like Cinderella," she remarked at the presentation ceremony. Mrs. Bush's inaugural ball attire—sapphire-blue gown, with a square-necked velvet bodice and a full satin skirt, and matching accessories—has now also joined other First Ladies' gowns in the Smithsonian's exhibition.

As HUSBAND AND FATHER, nearly every President has known the frustration, especially in periods of national stress, of trying to find enough time to be with his family.

When Garfield's son Harry was 17 and fell in love with the daughter of one of his father's best friends, a month passed before young Garfield was able to get the President alone to talk about it.

Eleanor Roosevelt wrote in her memoirs that at times the Roosevelt boys had to make appointments to see their father. On one occasion, she recalled, F.D.R. was so deep in an important document that he seemed unconscious of one son's account of a personal matter, and the young man left without getting his father's opinion. "I doubt if the public realizes," Mrs. Roosevelt commented, "the price that the whole family pays in curtailment of opportunity to live a close family life."

One of the most endearing aspects of life in the Executive Mansion can be glimpsed from the hundreds of stories that have come down through the years about the many children who have lived, and sometimes grown up, in the big white house where something new and exciting is always happening.

The very young ones were usually grandchildren, since few men

CLINEDINST PHOTOGRAPH, LIBRARY OF CONGRESS (BELOW); COURTESY MARTHENA HARRISON WILLIAMS

Models of decorum here, grandchildren of Benjamin Harrison enjoy a party in the second-floor nursery of the White House. Marthena Harrison reaches tentatively into a bowl, Mary McKee tastes a cookie, and Benjamin (Baby) McKee watches from his rocker. Presiding: the President's daughter, Mrs. James Robert McKee (left), and his daughter-in-law, Mrs. Russell B. Harrison. At right, President Wilson cradles his first granddaughter, Ellen Wilson McAdoo, in 1915.

have reached the top rung of the political ladder in early years. And the first of all the children whose shouts and laughter echoed through the mansion's broad corridors was the 4-year-old granddaughter of John and Abigail Adams.

Little Susanna arrived in November 1800 in the carriage bringing her grandmother, who was belatedly joining President Adams in the dank, unfinished building. The little girl distressed her grandparents soon afterward by developing whooping cough, but she recovered, and lived to tell her own small granddaughter Susanna of her adventures in the White House.

Jefferson's eight years in the Presidency were cheered and brightened by the visits of his married daughters, Martha Randolph and Maria Eppes. On one of these visits, in the winter of 1805, Mrs. Randolph gave birth to her eighth child—named James Madison Randolph—the first baby born in the Executive Mansion.

Jefferson was a devoted father and a fond grandfather, always ready for a race on the lawn or a romp inside with his daughters' bright youngsters. In her chronicles of early Washington life, Margaret Bayard Smith recalled his remark to her when she mentioned the amusement that children afforded adults. "Yes," Jefferson said, "it is only with them that a grave man can play the fool."

THOUGH ANDREW and Rachel Jackson never had children of their own, the widowed President surrounded himself with Rachel's visiting nieces and nephews and their offspring. Three of the six or more youngsters usually on hand were born in the White House. These three were children of Rachel's nephew Andrew Jackson Donelson, who stayed with the President as his private secretary, and his lovely wife, Emily, who served as Jackson's official hostess.

"Uncle Andrew," as the children called the President, often attended personally to the needs and wants of his adopted family; he rolled their baby carriages through the halls, comforted them in teething, and frequently joined in their games.

Golden-haired Mary Emily Donelson wrote long afterward about a happy Christmas season that she spent with the President, and of a party that Jackson gave for the youngsters, their playmates, and other Washington children.

Though the world knew him as a man of "iron will and fierce, ungovernable temper . . . ," she said, "he was the gentlest, tenderest, most patient of men at his own fireside."

The most photographed Presidential grandchild of the 19th century must have been "Baby McKee," who lived in the White House with grandfather Benjamin Harrison and his four-generation family during

"Mrs. Adams is winding silk from several hundred silkworms that she has ▷ been rearing," President John Quincy Adams recorded in his diary on June 23, 1828. Hot water dissolves the gum that cements the cocoons' filaments.

PAINTING BY LOUIS S. GLANZMAN, 1970

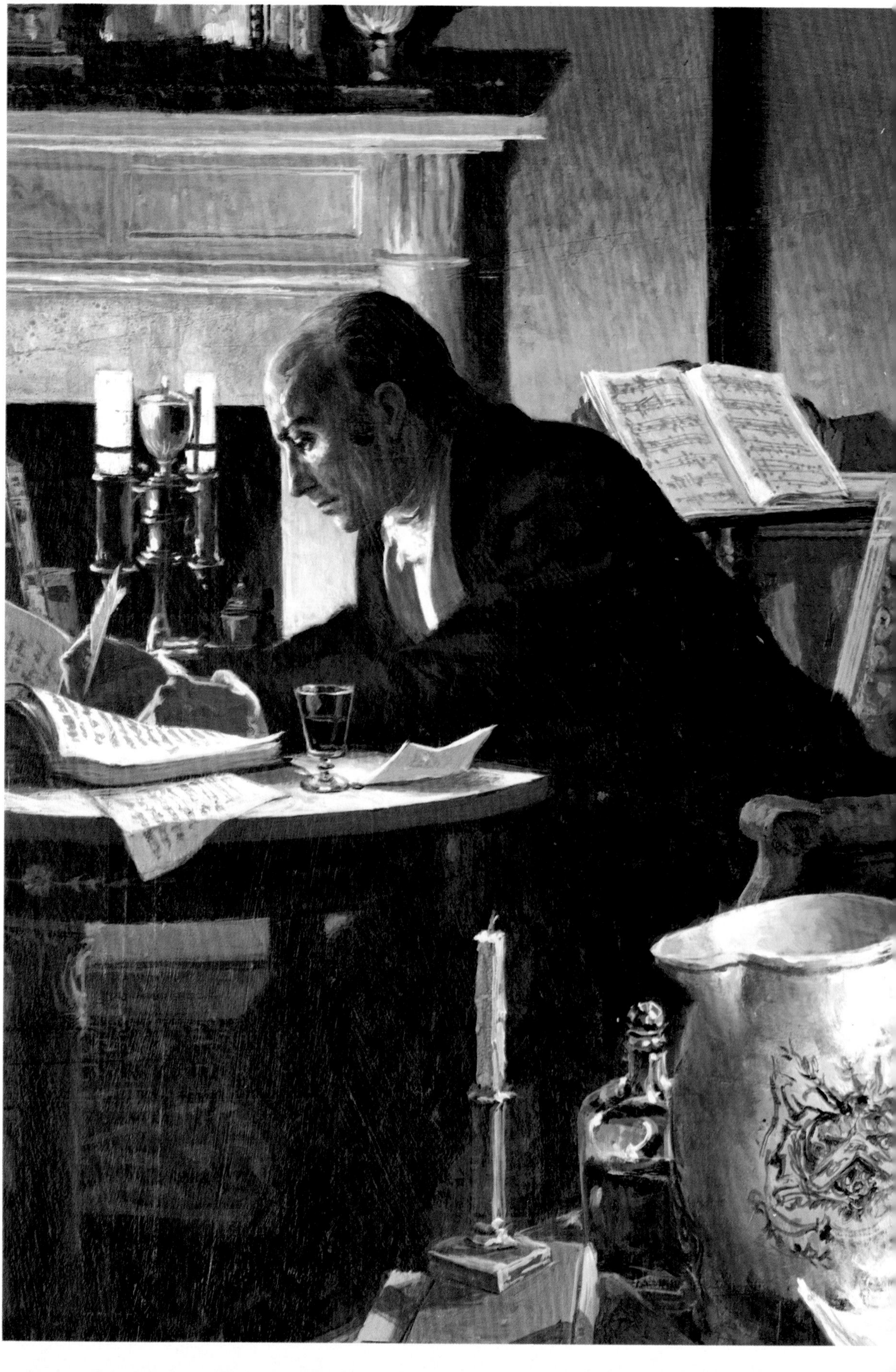

the early 1890's. Among the numerous members of the ménage, which included parents, grandparents, aunt, uncle, cousins, and great-grandfather, mischievous little Benjamin gained a reputation with the press as the President's favorite who could do no wrong.

Professional and amateur photographers were just then discovering George Eastman's new, easy-to-operate Kodak box camera—one of the first to use roll film—and they haunted the grounds, hoping to get pictures of little Benjamin. Soon, published photographs showed the active and appealing youngster as he played with his dog, led the Marine Band, or drove his own goat cart about the grounds.

The goat, called "His Whiskers" by the coachman, once ran away with Baby McKee, giving reporters one of their best stories about him. As His Whiskers darted off with the boy and raced down the White House driveway onto Pennsylvania Avenue, the portly President himself, dressed in top hat and frock coat, followed in hot pursuit.

With such a start in the 1890's, illustrated news coverage of the younger members of the Chief Executive's family has never slackened.

Roosevelt grandchildren, 13 in all, gather with Eleanor and F.D.R. on his fourth inaugural, January 20, 1945. Their grandmother Eleanor had slides, sandboxes, and swings built for the younger children on the south lawn.

Stories and pictures of Franklin Roosevelt's grandchildren Anna Eleanor and Curtis Dall made their nicknames, "Sistie" and "Buzzie," household words throughout the country during their stay in the White House. In January 1945, near the end of Roosevelt's 12-year administration, all 13 of his grandchildren attended his historic fourth inauguration—the largest group of grandchildren ever assembled at the Executive Mansion.

In their time, President and Mrs. Eisenhower delighted in the visits of their four grandchildren, David, Barbara Anne, Susan, and Mary Jean. Though none of these children of John and Barbara Eisenhower actually lived in the White House, the youngest, Mary Jean, was christened in the Blue Room, and all found plenty of toys and playground equipment on hand for their amusement.

The children called their grandmother "Mimi," and a revealing story shows how they regarded Grandfather Eisenhower. Someone had asked small David his name. "Dwight David Eisenhower," he replied. "Then who's that?" probed the questioner, pointing to the President. "That's Ike," said the boy.

It may surprise many who recall pictures of Abraham Lincoln's lined and aging face that he and his wife, 52 and 43 respectively, were among the younger Presidential couples, and that they were the first to bring to the White House a child of their own who was under 10. Thomas, or "Tad," was 7, William 10, and their brother Robert, who would be off at college most of the time, 17, when Lincoln and his family arrived in Washington from Illinois to become part of the nation's most tragic era.

Abraham and Mary Lincoln were loving and indulgent parents who often said, "Let the children have a good time." This the children did, and the President's friends and colleagues quite probably felt at times that he was too permissive when he failed to punish Tad for bombard-

ing the door with his toy cannon during a Cabinet meeting, or when the boy stopped his father's callers to sell refreshments and wheedle money for war charities at stands he set up at the mansion.

But the President found Tad's pranks a welcome relief from sorrow and responsibility; and both Lincoln and his wife took pride in Tad's generous nature, as well as in the talent that gentle, cheerful Willie revealed in the verses and short speeches he composed.

Lincoln thoroughly enjoyed, too, the physical activity of a good wrestling match with his boys, and he encouraged them in the fun of collecting and raising pets of various kinds, including dogs, ponies, and goats. When one of the goats disappeared, he wrote a whimsical letter saying that "poor Nanny" had last been seen "chewing her little cud, on the middle of Tad's bed. . . ."

A devastating blow came to the family when Willie developed a severe fever and died soon afterward, on February 20, 1862.

The President shouldered his grief with his other burdens, but high-strung, erratic Mary Lincoln was inconsolable. She turned to spiritualism in the hope of receiving a message from beyond the grave, and arranged at least one session with a popular medium of the day at the Soldiers' Home—the Lincolns' "summer White House."

For a while Mrs. Lincoln believed her lost boy had returned. "He comes to me every night," she told her sister, "and stands at the foot of my bed, with the same sweet, adorable smile. . . ." Later she wrote, ". . . the loved & idolized being, comes no more."

Some insisted that Lincoln himself attended one of the spiritualist meetings, though it was never made clear whether this was to please his wife, to satisfy his own curiosity, born of a streak of mysticism, or to show up the medium's tricks. One story had the President joking about conflicting suggestions offered him by "Napoleon," "Lafayette," and other spirits on the conduct of the war.

"Their talk and advice," he reportedly said, "sound very much like the talk of my Cabinet."

On the eve of Union victory early in April 1865, Lincoln described a strange dream to his wife and a good friend. In the dream, he said, he was awakened from a deep sleep by a "pitiful sobbing." Getting up, he followed the wailing sound to the East Room, and there he found a catafalque, surrounded by mourners. On it he saw a still figure shrouded in funeral garb, the face covered.

"The President," one of the soldiers standing in the honor guard whispered to Lincoln, ". . . killed by an assassin."

Within two weeks, Abraham Lincoln had been shot by John Wilkes Booth in Ford's Theatre. In the East Room, Lincoln's body lay on a catafalque, surrounded by mourners as foretold by the dream.

In a room above, Mary Lincoln lay prostrated by grief. While Tad and Robert sought to comfort her, they could hear the sound of weeping from long lines of people passing the bier to pay their last respects.

President and Mrs. Grant, the next couple to arrive at the Executive Mansion with young children of their own, were fortunate in leading one of the happiest and most normal of family lives in the history of the White House.

The Grants' affectionate and outgoing children—three sons and a daughter named Nellie—ranged in age from 11 to 18. The middle son, Ulysses Simpson Jr., was called "Buck" because he was born in the Buckeye State of Ohio. Both he and his older brother, Frederick,

HANK WALKER, LIFE MAGAZINE © TIME, INC.

Storybook romance between David Eisenhower and Julie Nixon captured the country's imagination. The couple met as shy 8-year-olds at Ike's second inaugural (above). On December 22, 1968, they were married in New York.

worked for the President as confidential secretaries during Grant's second term in office.

Fred, a graduate of West Point, married Ida Maria Honoré in October 1874, though the wedding was not held at the White House as Nellie's had been. Later the couple came to live in the mansion, and here a daughter was born and named Julia, after her grandmother.

One of the liveliest and warmest accounts of the Grants comes from the fun-loving youngest son, Jesse. In his book of reminiscences, *In the Days of My Father, General Grant,* he told of his joy in the gift of a small but powerful telescope, which he used to study the heavens. He recalled the gatherings of neighborhood friends who "flocked to the White House . . . the largest and best playground available." The "lot was our playground, in good weather," he wrote, " . . . the big, airy basement . . . was reserved for rain or storm."

Jesse also became an ardent stamp collector. In his impatience to

WHITE HOUSE PHOTOGRAPH

receive an order that he had paid for with $5 out of his savings, he appealed to his father, suggesting that the dealer be prodded by a letter from the Secretary of State, the Secretary of War, or Kelly, a policeman on White House duty. The matter was solemnly debated at a Cabinet meeting with Jesse pleading his case. It was finally decided to have Kelly write the following: "I am a Capitol Policeman. I can arrest anybody, anywhere, at any time, for anything. I want you to send those stamps to Jesse Grant right at once."

The stamps came.

Wrote Jesse in memory of his family: "The love of my parents for each other and their devotion to us children made no impression on me then. I had never known anything different. Appreciation and understanding come to me now, filling me with content."

As had Grant, both Rutherford B. Hayes and James A. Garfield brought to the Executive Mansion in turn a warmhearted, close-knit family. Each included four boys and a girl. Moreover, the two families were old friends, linked by common Ohio origins and Congressional service in Washington.

Fanny Hayes and Mollie Garfield, both 14, sat together at Garfield's inauguration, behind the mother of the President-elect—the first mother to see her son take the oath of office. Mollie continued her friendship with Fanny after the family, including Grandmother Garfield, moved into the mansion. When Mollie gave a luncheon for ten young girls, she

Julie and David Eisenhower often visited the White House during her father's Presidency. They now live near Philadelphia. She has written a book about her mother, and David has completed one volume of a biography of his grandfather.

remembered her obligations as a hostess in the White House, and seated Fanny, as the daughter of a past President, on her right.

With Garfield's accession to the Presidency, his two older sons, Harry and James, stayed at the White House, studying there under a private tutor instead of completing the remaining months of their prep-school terms. Thus they, too, happened to be with the rest of the family, along with Mollie and the two younger boys, Irvin and Abram, during most of the last six months of their father's life.

For the rest of their lives, Harry and James Garfield would look back in horror upon the morning of July 2, 1881, when they and the President were planning to join Mrs. Garfield, who was then vacationing in Long Branch, New Jersey.

The two boys were in high spirits at the prospect of the trip, and President Garfield, a large and active man despite his bookish bent, joined them in a bit of horseplay before they all departed for the Washington depot of the Baltimore and Potomac Railway. Less than an hour later, an office-seeking fanatic, Charles Guiteau, fired two shots at Garfield as he entered the waiting room. Garfield fell; physicians rushed to the scene, and a horse-drawn police ambulance soon returned the gravely wounded President to the White House.

For more than two months, Garfield battled for life in his second-floor bedroom at the mansion, while his wife and children waited and prayed. Outside the gates, frequent bulletins kept the public informed of the condition of the man in the sickroom. A metal-detecting device developed by Alexander Graham Bell was used in an attempt to locate the bullet, but the effort failed because of interference from the bed's steel springs.

In the hope that sea air might help cure the President, he was finally transferred by train—with every precaution taken to prevent jolting—to the ocean resort of Elberon at Long Branch, New Jersey.

But no air could combat the infection that had developed. Garfield died on September 19, and his body was carried directly to the Capitol to lie in state in the Rotunda. It was the only time in history that a President who had died in office did not lie in state in the East Room.

The only President's child born in the mansion was Esther Cleveland, the second daughter of Grover and Frances Cleveland. Esther's sister Ruth, who had arrived during the interlude between Cleveland's two terms, was almost 2 years old at the time of Esther's birth in 1893. Before the President's second term ended, another little girl, Marion, was born at the Clevelands' summer home in Massachusetts.

"The Cleveland children were . . . much beloved by everyone around the place," wrote durable Chief Usher Ike Hoover, who would serve in ten administrations. "We often wished that more of them had been born in the White House. . . ."

The public seemed to feel much the same way about the three pretty little girls. Gifts and advice on how to rear them poured into the White House from all over the country.

Staid rooms resound to boyish laughter as Presidential children turn the White House into an arena for a boisterous game. The Garfield boys—Irvin, 11, and Abram, 9—maneuver cumbersome velocipedes during an East Room pillow fight. At left, Tad and Willie Lincoln improvise a quieter game—a costume drama in the White House attic. In this painting, Willie wears some of his mother's cast-off clothes, Tad the uniform and trappings of a Union brigadier general.

One Washington boy organized what he called an honor guard for Ruth. Marching his young company up to the door, he asked for, and received, an interview with the President. Cleveland regretted he was too busy to review the troops, but he delegated the role to Mrs. Cleveland, who complied with pleasure.

Another, less pleasant, incident occurred when a group of curious visitors gathered around Ruth and her nurse during an outing on the grounds. One of the women picked up the child and passed her around to the accompaniment of pats and kisses.

The episode so alarmed Mrs. Cleveland that from then on the gates to the south lawn were closed to the public—an exclusion that resulted in cruel and baseless rumors that the child was deformed.

Four and a half years after the departure of the demure little Cleveland girls, the uninhibited children of Theodore Roosevelt came on with the force of a hurricane.

"A nervous person had no business around the White House in those days," observed Ike Hoover in describing their behavior. ". . . Places that had not seen a human being for years were now made alive with the howls and laughter of these newcomers. . . . Nothing was too sacred for their amusement and no place too good for a playroom."

Among other pranks, the five younger children—aged 3 to 14 when the Roosevelts arrived—slid down the stairways on trays stolen from the pantry, stalked the halls on stilts, and bicycled and skated on newly polished floors.

Their lovely, self-willed half sister, Alice, then 17, contributed to the uproar in her own way. She refused to go away to boarding school, but she later made trips around the country, as well as to Cuba, Puerto Rico, and the Orient. From shipboard in the Pacific came the story that "Princess Alice" had jumped, fully dressed, into the ship's pool.

Tad Lincoln, given a courtesy commission by Secretary of War Edwin M. Stanton, wears a colonel's uniform. His White House days ended after a black-draped drum (opposite) sounded at his father's funeral; many citizens hung mourning ribbons in their windows.

"I can do one of two things," the President once said. "I can be President of the United States, or I can control Alice."

The Roosevelt children also kept a small zoo of pets that included a badger, a bear, raccoons, cats, dogs, rats, guinea pigs, snakes, and a calico pony named Algonquin. When Archie had the measles, his brothers entertained him by leading the pony into his second-floor bedroom, after riding up in the President's elevator.

When the youngest child, Quentin, grew old enough, he was sent to a nearby public school, and he often brought his pals home to add to the commotion. One of these friends, Earle Looker, many years later wrote a book called *The White House Gang*. In it he described the hilarious adventures of the boys and the quick and just punishment meted out by the President after such antics as the spattering of Andrew Jackson's portrait with spitballs.

T. R., as the gang called him—not disrespectfully but with a mixture of affection and awe—had an amazing knowledge of the interests and needs of active children. When official business was slow, he sometimes joined the youngsters for games in the White House attic. On one such occasion, as the President was about to catch up with a boy he was chasing, young Earle turned out the light. A crash followed, and when Earle found the switch again, he saw Roosevelt holding his head and leaning against a post, from which a nail protruded shockingly close to the height of his eyes.

"I'm quite all right," he told the contrite boys, "but never, n-e-v-e-r, *never* again, turn off a light when anybody is near a post!"

Mrs. Roosevelt managed to preside with grace and calm over her large, boisterous group of children, and T. R. once summed up his feelings in a letter to their son Kermit: "I don't think that any family has ever enjoyed the White House more than we have."

TEN MORE ADMINISTRATIONS would follow that of Grover Cleveland before the cry of a President's infant was again heard inside the Executive Mansion. Then, early in 1961, came John and Jacqueline Kennedy with their 2-month-old baby, John Jr., and his engaging sister, Caroline, 3 years old.

Soon newspaper and magazine editors were publishing stories and pictures of the youngsters' third-floor playroom where the Eisenhower grandchildren had romped not long before; of the new tree house, swings, and other playground equipment behind south-lawn shrubbery; of Caroline's pet canary Robin, her pony Macaroni, and her dog Pushinka, the gift of Soviet Premier Nikita Khrushchev.

Multiplying anecdotes told how "John-John" had refused to greet the Grand Duchess of Luxembourg because he had not been given his usual cookie and ginger ale; how Caroline had presented India's Prime Minister Jawaharlal Nehru with a rose for his buttonhole; and what she said when reporters asked what her father was doing. "Oh, he's upstairs with his shoes and socks off," she said, "not doing anything." As a child of the Space Age, Caroline Kennedy made news again when she asked John Glenn not about his pioneering flight around the earth but about another orbital test with chimpanzees. "Where's the monkey?" she asked the astronaut.

By restricting photographs and limiting access to her children, Mrs. Kennedy sought to protect them from the effects of so much concentrated attention. She established a kindergarten at home, as had Mrs. Cleveland, so that Caroline and little John could play with children of their own age, away from the public eye.

Lack of personal privacy is an old complaint of Presidents and their wives. Certainly no couple suffered more from it than did the Clevelands on their honeymoon in 1886, when the "ghouls of the press," as Cleveland later called them, followed the newlyweds to a lodge at a Maryland mountain resort. Equipped with spyglasses and cameras,

Florence Harding with Laddie Boy.

Baby McKee holds the reins of His Whiskers, a goat presented to him by grand-

Millie, Ranger, and Mrs. Bush watch the President's helicopter land.

Mrs. Coolidge, raccoon Rebecca.

Him and Her, the Johnson beagles.

President Wilson's sheep crop White House lawns during World War I.

father Benjamin Harrison.   *F.D.R.'s dog, Fala, begs a handout.*   *Amy Carter and Misty Malarky Ying Yang.*

Caroline Kennedy rides Macaroni across the south grounds.   *Nancy Reagan's dog, Rex.*

Theodore Roosevelt, Jr., macaw Eli.   *White House policeman holds Algonquin's reins for Quentin Roosevelt.*

the newsmen went to incredible lengths to get stories and pictures.

During the election campaign of 1888, scurrilous rumors of Cleveland's mistreatment of his young wife gained such wide circulation that Mrs. Cleveland issued an indignant denial.

"I can wish the women of our Country no greater blessing," she said, "than that their homes and lives may be as happy, and their husbands may be as kind, attentive, considerate and affectionate as mine."

Today, reporters are not permitted to badger the First Family as they sometimes did in the past. Nor can individual members of the public now enter the White House grounds without an official pass or previous clearance by authorities. Armed, highly trained men of the Executive Protective Service, a uniformed branch of the Secret Service, are stationed in gatehouses along the high iron fence and closely check the identity of all callers.

The Secret Service maintains various other security measures in carrying out its responsibility of guarding the life of the President—a responsibility given to it in 1901, after McKinley's assassination. Specific regulations followed; one of the most important requires Secret Service agents to remain near the Chief Executive at all times. The objective is to offer maximum safeguards with a minimum of interference, but many Presidents have grown restive under the attention.

While Taft conceded that the record of assassinations was such that

Caroline Kennedy and her infant brother, John Jr., arrive at the White House for the first time on February 4, 1961. The portrait at left has been published as one of Mrs. Cleveland and baby Marion, later Mrs. John Harlan Amen; Mrs. Amen, however, believed the portrait to show her sister Esther, born in the White House in 1893.

"Congress would be quite derelict" in disregarding it, he added that it was difficult for a Chief Executive "to avoid the feeling . . . that he was under surveillance rather than under protection."

Theodore Roosevelt wrote to a friend: "The secret service men are a very small but very necessary thorn in the flesh." Then he went on to express his belief that no effort could prevent an assault upon his life and quoted Lincoln's remark that "though it would be safer for a President to live in a cage, it would interfere with his business."

Since a 1917 law extended Secret Service protection to other family members, unmarried sons and daughters of Presidents have faced the choice of giving up dates or accepting the company—however discreet—of an agent of the Service.

John Coolidge's classmates at Amherst joked that John would have to "elope from his agent" if he wanted to marry anyone. And Margaret Truman in her book *Souvenir* gives an account of "the handicap the Secret Service offers to escorts and beaus." She had made up her mind, she wrote, not to marry while she lived in the White House. But she asked the reader "to consider the effect of saying good night to a boy at the door . . . in a blaze of floodlights, with a Secret Service man in attendance. There is not much you can do except shake hands, and that's no way to get engaged."

Subsequent legislation now requires the Secret Service to guard not

Susan Ford focuses on her father in the Oval Office as he reviews some of her work. Coached by White House staff photographer David Hume Kennerly, Susan began taking pictures for a photography class at Holton-Arms School. For her senior project, she submitted a portfolio of behind-the-scenes glimpses of life in the White House.

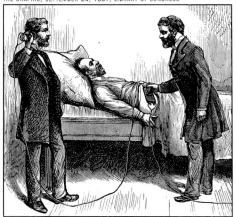

*With deep concern, but inadequate medical
resources, physicians wait with Mrs.
Garfield as the President struggles to re-
cover from a wound inflicted by an assassin
on July 2, 1881. A crowd gathers outside
the White House (top, left) awaiting the
medical bulletin issued each morning; a
mounted courier departs to inform the
Cabinet of the President's condition, and a
little girl brings a bouquet for the wounded
Chief Executive. Above, Alexander Graham
Bell, hoping to locate the bullet, listens
with the telephone-like receiver of
an electrical device he invented for detecting
metal; steel springs in the mattress inter-
fered. All efforts to save the President
failed, and he died on September 19, 1881.*

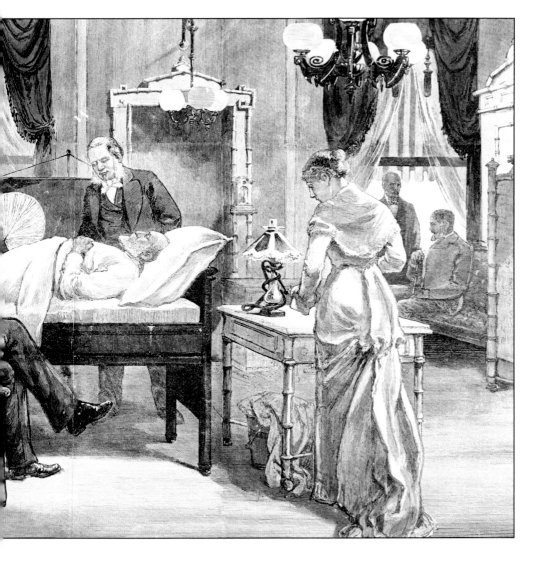

only the President and his family but also the President-elect, the Vice President, their families, as well as former Presidents, their widows and minor children, Presidential candidates, and top officials from abroad. The cost is great, but in these days of political terrorism and random violence, arguments for cutbacks have been easily overruled.

On March 30, 1981, another attempt to assassinate an American President again underscored Roosevelt's point that no amount of precautions can eliminate such attacks. Unnoticed by the crowd standing outside a leading hotel in the nation's Capital that day, a young man waited, handgun at the ready. When President Reagan emerged after a luncheon speech inside, a hail of bullets struck him, his press secretary, a Secret Service agent, and a Washington, D. C., policeman.

The President, at first unaware that he had been hit, was rushed to George Washington University Hospital. There, amid preparations for emergency surgery, he sought to relieve tensions by a spontaneous act of wit and courage that charmed the whole country.

"Honey, I forgot to duck," he told his wife on her arrival at the hospital. To the surgeons readying him for the operation, he quipped that he hoped they were Republicans. After more than three hours of surgery to remove the bullet, he cracked, "If I got this much attention in Hollywood, I'd never have left."

As the world knows now, the President made a remarkable recovery from his wound. The security officers survived to be honored for their bravery under fire. The press secretary, James S. Brady, who suffered the most serious injury, is showing marked improvement after extensive physical therapy.

The assailant—a 25-year-old drifter from Denver, Colorado, named John W. Hinckley, Jr.—was tried for the crime, and on June 22, 1982, was declared "not guilty by reason of insanity."

Today a detail of sharp-eyed men—augmented by women agents assigned to the job since 1978—has never been far from the Bush family since George Bush was elected to the Presidency in 1988.

DESPITE WHATEVER HAZARDS and lack of privacy our modern Presidents may endure, nothing could approach the shocking conditions that prevailed in family living arrangements until the beginning of the 20th century. The executive offices and family apartment shared space in the mansion itself. For much of the time, these rooms occupied opposite ends of the same floor.

In those days, a multitude of callers, ranging from tradesmen and patronage seekers to Cabinet officers and foreign dignitaries, streamed into and out of the north entrance. Some lounged as they waited in rooms on the state floor; others trudged up the public stairway to see the President or members of his staff.

To avoid the often rough crowds, some of the older and more delicate wives of Presidents seldom ventured out of their west-side family quarters. One of these was the first Mrs. Tyler. An invalid from a stroke

GOODBYE ALL, GOODBYE, IT IS GOD'S WAY, HIS WILL NOT OURS BE DONE.

A grieving figure, the stricken nation personified, appears atop William McKinley's mourning ribbon. Anarchist Leon Czolgosz approached the President and shot him as he stood in a receiving line at the Pan American Exposition at Buffalo, New York, on September 6, 1901.

suffered before she came to the White House, Letitia Tyler managed to run the household from her bedroom. This she did so efficiently and "so quietly," wrote her admiring daughter-in-law, Priscilla, "that you can't tell when she does it."

Mrs. Zachary Taylor was another White House homebody. She received visitors only in her own quarters and limited her guests almost entirely to close friends and to relatives from the South.

Mrs. Taylor was a reluctant First Lady. The General, she felt, deserved a rest after 40 years of active duty that included service in the War of 1812, in skirmishes with frontier Indians, and in the Mexican War. During the election year of 1848, Taylor told supporters that his wife prayed nightly for his defeat. If he was unlucky enough to win the office, she had declared, it would shorten his life.

Mrs. Taylor's dark prophecy came true just 16 months after her husband's inauguration. On July 4, 1850, the President sat for hours under the hot sun at a celebration on the grounds of the unfinished Washington Monument. Overheated and exhausted, he became ill of what was then called cholera morbus—the result, legend would say, of his having consumed too much iced milk and raw cherries.

Five days later, Zachary Taylor was dead. His grieving widow, secluded in her apartment, could hear the sounds of his office staff making way for the next occupants, and she could feel the vibrations of hammering as workmen assembled a catafalque in the East Room.

She could not bear to attend the ceremony, but she was forced to listen to its accompaniment, a sympathetic eyewitness reported, "as one band after another blared the funeral music . . . and the heavy guns boomed . . . to announce the final parting."

In later administrations, as executive responsibilities grew heavier and the number of visitors increased, Presidential families faced ever greater inconveniences. A member of President Garfield's staff recalled in his memoirs that a mere acquaintance of the family "pushed himself in past the doors that marked the private domain . . . and took his afternoon siesta upon the most comfortable sofa he could find."

President Benjamin Harrison's wife, in an 1889 interview, complained that she was "being made a circus of . . I've been a show, the whole family's been a show since Mr. Harrison was elected," she said. "All last fall I sat in my sewing room and watched the procession of feet pass across the parlour floor wearing their path into the nap, and disappear like the trail of a caravan into the General's room beyond. Day by day, I watched the path grow wider and deeper. . . . But I don't propose to be made a circus of forever! If there's any privacy to be found in the White House, I propose to find it. . . ."

Mrs. Harrison's solution to the problem called for Congress to adopt one of three drastic measures, for which she presented detailed architectural plans. The simplest of these would have provided the President with a separate residence and remodeled the mansion for entertaining and executive business only. The second design proposed the addition

Mourning badge—a miniature photograph trimmed in black velvet— depicts President Warren G. Harding. He died in San Francisco on August 2, 1923, after suffering a heart attack.

of wings to be used for office and guest suites. The most elaborate of the suggestions was to extend the house into a fantastic four-sided palace enclosing a huge court and fountains.

Though Congress rejected Mrs. Harrison's projects, it did appropriate $35,000 for essential housecleaning and repairs to the deteriorating old house. Moreover, airing the need for reasonable family privacy and adequate office space helped pave the way for the future construction of wings on the west and east sides of the mansion.

FROM THE BEGINNING, each President and his family have created a highly individual home within the Executive Mansion by furnishing and embellishing it in their own taste.

Dolley Madison expressed her warm and vibrant personality in decorating the Presidential quarters with bright yellow draperies and upholstery. Sedate and proper Lucy Hayes had her bedroom walls "tinted pale blue, with panels of light gray and pink," as described by a woman correspondent permitted the rare privilege of seeing the Hayeses' private apartment in the 1870's.

Abigail Fillmore, a onetime schoolteacher who had met her husband-to-be when they attended school together, obtained Congressional funds for the first official library in the Executive Mansion. With a dictionary, histories, sets of Dickens, Thackeray, and other works, she filled the bookshelves installed in the upstairs sitting room. There, she and President Fillmore spent many quiet evenings reading and chatting, while their young daughter, Mary Abigail, played the piano or harp.

Equally revealing possessions have moved in and out of the White House with each successive family. With the Tafts, for instance, came the President's many lawbooks, recalling his long and distinguished legal career capped eventually by his appointment as Chief Justice of the United States.

The erudite Hoovers brought many mementos from their world travels. South American rugs, Oriental art, caged songbirds—and books in various languages, including their own translation from Latin of an important 16th-century volume on mining. All of which helped Lou Hoover transform the broad, bare hall on the second floor into an inviting reception area for guests.

Majestic columns of the South Portico frame Mrs. Dwight D. Eisenhower on the balcony as she waves a birthday greeting to her husband, 70 years old on October 14, 1960. After some 30 moves in 36 years of Army travels, the Eisenhowers lived longer together in the White House than anyplace else.

To the White House from Hyde Park, New York, Franklin and Eleanor Roosevelt shipped some of their sturdy handcrafted furniture and a wheelchair that would carry the President along the family corridor.

During the Trumans' time, the second floor held three pianos—appropriate symbols of the close harmony that characterized the family from Independence, Missouri. One piano stood in the oval room that was then the President's study; Margaret practiced on another in her sitting room, where she also kept her record collection, while a third—a spinet in the hall—was often used for duets.

A few years later, when friends of President Eisenhower visited him in the upstairs oval room, which he, too, used as a study, they found

displayed there a fascinating array of military and civilian awards, decorations, swords, and other gifts presented by world leaders. In his book *The White House Years*, the President wrote that he received visitors in the study "informally in the evening, whenever a somewhat homier atmosphere than could be obtained in my office was desirable." His "personal mementos of a fairly long life," he added, ". . . were kept there for a temporary period only, and later were transferred to a suitable museum—the Smithsonian, the Library of Congress, or the museum which bears my name in Abilene, Kansas."

After the Eisenhowers and the President's prized souvenirs went their separate ways, the changing scenes on the family floor continued to mirror, in colors and furnishings, tastes and activities of each new group of White House occupants.

Mrs. Eisenhower's feminine and frilly decor, with its "Mamie pink" accents in flowered slipcovers and draperies, gave way to Mrs. Kennedy's light-blue curtains and blue-and-white furnishings that showed to advantage against plain off-white walls in the private bedroom and sitting-room areas.

American period pieces, French antiques, and valuable art objects began to appear in various places: the sitting halls that share the wide corridor; the Queens' and Lincoln Bedrooms, where visiting royalty had slept; and what was called the Treaty Room, then decorated in Victorian style. They gave visible evidence of Jacqueline Kennedy's program to restore to the White House furnishings that awaken a feeling of the historic past.

The Yellow Oval Room on the second floor has had the same color and Louis XVI furnishings, and has served the same function, for the last seven administrations. Mrs. Kennedy turned this room into a formal drawing room, and it has proved to be the most suitable place in the house to entertain state guests before dinners or luncheons given in their honor.

With the arrival of the Johnson family, Mrs. Johnson put her own signature on the look and use of the second-floor apartments. In her mainly green-and-yellow bedroom (symbolic, perhaps, of her project for the greening and beautification of Washington and the country) she set up a cozy working space, in which she dictated letters and speeches, and planned and directed her many activities.

"My house," John Kennedy, Jr., called the President's massive desk. He liked to hide behind its secret door while his father worked. Above, President Lincoln leafs through a photograph album with his youngest son, Tad.

Down the hall—in rooms that had lately known the toys of the Kennedy children—the Johnsons' teenage girls, Luci and Lynda, had their bedrooms until marriage took them both to homes of their own. And when President Nixon brought his family to the White House in 1969, his daughter Tricia moved into the suite that had been Lynda and Luci's. The following year, Tricia took television viewers on the first public showing of many of the rooms in the family living quarters.

The tour started on the balcony overlooking the south lawn, with its lovely view of the Washington Monument and the Jefferson Memorial. Included were glimpses of the family dining and sitting rooms, and of the guest room called the Queens' Bedroom because five queens have slept there during state visits.

Tricia pointed out her mother's sitting room, in which she read and answered her mail, and the piano her father liked to play. She also described an incident in which Nixon built the flames so high in the fireplace of his private study adjoining the Lincoln Bedroom that an alarm sent White House fire fighters rushing to the scene. There, they found him placidly writing a speech before the open fire, which, Tricia explained, was one of his great pleasures. In fact, she added, the President liked a cozy fire so much that he would light one even in warm weather and turn on the air conditioning.

After the Carters moved in, ten-year-old Amy occupied the bedroom that had been Caroline Kennedy's, then Luci Johnson's, then Tricia Nixon's. The youngest of the Carter offspring, Amy was by far the best known. Her tree house in the gnarled old cedar on the south lawn, her delight in reading, her violin lessons, pets, and school friends became part of the continuing White House small-fry chronicles that began with Susanna, granddaughter of John and Abigail Adams.

P RESIDENT AND MRS. REAGAN put their stamp on the second-floor family quarters, as well as on the expanded living space that was added to the third floor during the Truman reconstruction of 1948-52. Most of this floor was then divided into bedroom, bath, and sitting-room apartments, which are available today for family members and personal guests. The remaining area serves as space for storage and housekeeping, with one room reserved for recreation. Mrs. Reagan's work on these floors completed the refurbishing project begun by Mrs. Kennedy in 1961.

Mrs. Reagan sought private donations for her projects, and they eventually totalled more than $800,000. The money came from all over the country and ranged from a child's one-dollar contribution to ten thousand dollars or more from wealthy donors. The donations were largely spent on basic renovation, and for restoration of certain valuable—and sometimes historically priceless—articles that had been in storage. "Retrieving them was an exciting treasure hunt," said Mrs. Reagan of the scores of large and small objects that she and her decorator rediscovered and put back in use.

Some of the most striking changes were made on the third floor. Its wide central hall offers space in which to display refinished, reupholstered, and regilded 19th-century Federal furniture, as well as Currier & Ives prints, decorative objects, and sculpture. Of special interest to historians and antique buffs is a lacquered table that is in use in the sitting room at the east end of this floor. The table was brought as a gift to President Buchanan in 1860 by the first diplomatic mission sent from Imperial Japan to the United States.

Commanding the scene from the Center Hall of the second floor stands a gleaming mahogany desk, surrounded by pieces of furniture from the 18th and early 19th centuries. This octagonal pedestal writing desk, called a partners' desk, was made in England during the late 18th century. It can be separated into two parts, or combined—as in its present use—to make a central divider.

The Reagan redecoration focused chiefly on the second and third floors. But one elegant wanderer purchased by Monroe in 1817—a French Empire sofa—was returned to the Blue Room on the state floor.

Rolling caisson, followed by the President's flag, a riderless horse, and an assemblage of world leaders, bears John F. Kennedy from the White House to St. Matthew's Cathedral on November 25, 1963. An assassin had felled the President three days before in Dallas.

Like any other happily married couple, President and Mrs. Reagan enjoy sharing a quiet evening at home. When in the White House, they often ate dinner while watching the news in the President's second-floor study. This room contained furniture from their California home and a number of mementos, including the desk lamp made from a fire chief's silver horn.

Sold at auction just before the Civil War, this gilded sofa, curved to fit the room, came home in 1978, only to be stored again. Finally reclaimed and re-covered with blue silk, it joined seven of the original matching chairs.

For all its splendor, the White House is still the temporary family home of the man the people have elected to be their leader. George and Barbara Bush, like others before them, have brought many of their own belongings to make their quarters warm and welcoming with familiar furniture and ornaments.

President Bush chose as his private office a room that often served as the Cabinet Room before the Presidential offices were moved to the West Wing. Called the Monroe Room after Mrs. Hoover decorated it with reproductions of the French furniture ordered by President Monroe, it was renamed the Treaty Room in 1961 when it was redecorated to resemble the Cabinet Room at the time of Grant.

The President's Office contains a comfortable combination of modern furniture and American antiques and reproductions. The oak desk was given to President Hayes by Queen Victoria, and has been used by almost every President since then. It is made of timbers from H.M.S. *Resolute* when she was broken up. The ship had been abandoned north of the Arctic Circle, was recovered, refitted, and returned to Queen Victoria as a gesture of American friendship.

The most important work of art in the room is George P. A. Healy's "The Peacemakers." Painted in 1868, it shows President Lincoln meeting with General Grant and other military advisers during the siege of Petersburg, Virginia. Other American paintings and sculpture—many with a Western theme—are displayed in the room; and George Bush personally chose a Winslow Homer watercolor of the Maine coast "Surf at Prout's Neck."

Dozens of framed photographs of the President's family are in the office. Other personal items include a basket filled with stuffed toys for the 12 grandchildren to play with when they visit and a collection of tiny toy soldiers on the mantel.

The room next to the Yellow Oval Room on the second floor has always been part of the Presidential families' private apartments. Furnished now as a family sitting room, its focal point is a needlepoint rug. Barbara Bush spent nine years completing its eight panels, each 18 inches by 8 feet, taking them with her on travels through 17 countries and 36 states. Assembled, the rug depicts a lily pond framed by flowers and small animals. Part of the Bushes' collection of Chinese porcelain is displayed here; the room also contains two Chinese tapestries, made of blue silk with white-and-gold embroidery.

President and Mrs. Bush have five children: George Walker, John Ellis (Jeb), Neil Mallon, Marvin Pierce, and Dorothy Walker (Doro).

George W. and his wife, Laura, live in Dallas. They have two daughters, Jenna and Barbara. Jeb and Columba Bush live in Miami with their three children: George Prescott, Noelle, and John Ellis, Jr. Neil and his wife, Sharon, have three children: Lauren, Pierce, and Ashley. They live in Denver. Marvin and his wife, Margaret, have a daughter, Marshall, and a son, Walker, and live in Alexandria, Virginia. Dorothy Bush LeBlond lives in Bethesda, Maryland, with her two children, Samuel and Nancy Ellis (Ellie).

All of the Bush children and grandchildren have visited the White House, sometimes staying in one of the apartments on the third floor or enjoying the thrill of sleeping in the Lincoln Bedroom or the Queens' Bedroom on the second floor.

EVERY PRESIDENT'S FAMILY takes its place in the flow of historic continuity, while undergoing the turns and twists of its own life. During the Bush tenure, few changes were made in the decor and furnishings of the ground floor. One that followed tradition, however, was the installation in the corridor of a portrait of the previous First Lady: Aaron Shikler's painting of Nancy Davis Reagan.

Before Theodore Roosevelt separated his office from his home, the basement of the mansion served as a workmen's area, cluttered with buckets and lumber, and defaced with pipes run through the walls. Today, this wide corridor shows off 19th-century American furnishings and displays on its walls a gallery of First Ladies' portraits.

The Bushes make frequent use of the handsome rooms that line the

Rosalynn Carter greets sightseers on a morning tour of the White House.

Pat Nixon applauds during a

Betty Ford greets a blind March of Dimes Poster Child.

Grace Coolidge cuts a cake honoring the Visiting

With help from a school group, Lady Bird Johnson plants a tree on the north lawn.

Nancy Reagan presides over

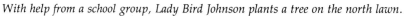

"Summer in the Parks" program.

Barbara Bush gives a lifesaving award to a school Safety Patrol member.

Nurses Association.

a conference on drug abuse.

First Ladies, in addition to their ceremonial duties as official hostess of the White House, increasingly pursue interests of their own. Eleanor Roosevelt championed the underprivileged and minority groups. Lady Bird Johnson initiated a national beautification program, which is renewed each year by blossoming trees and flower gardens. Pat Nixon emphasized volunteer work and played an active role in acquiring many furnishings and art objects for the White House Collection. Betty Ford strongly backed the Equal Rights Amendment. Rosalynn Carter addressed problems of the mentally ill, the elderly, and inner-city dwellers. Nancy Reagan joined the battle against drug abuse, particularly among the young. Volunteerism is a way of life for Barbara Bush. With minimum ceremony, she works in the community on varied projects: feeding the homeless, encouraging reading, and helping in a home for the aged; her satisfaction comes from "seeing that I can make a difference."

Britain's Queen Elizabeth, wife of George VI, rides with Eleanor Roosevelt.

corridor. The Library, with 19th-century portraits of Indian chiefs, and the Map Room, where F.D.R. kept up with World War II progress, are especially suitable for interviews, videotaping, and small conferences.

Behind such scenes and events, the men and women who have lived in the Executive Mansion have known the same happiness and frustration, pride and misery that come to all of us.

Every night, the gruff and lonely warrior, Andrew Jackson, performed a tender ritual. After removing the treasured miniature of his dead wife, Rachel, which he carried next to his heart, he would place it on the bedside table near her worn and faded Bible, so that he might see her face first on awakening in the morning.

In another of the family rooms, frail Eliza Johnson, devoted wife of Andrew for 41 years, rocked and sewed as she awaited word of the Senate vote at her husband's impeachment trial. "I knew he'd be acquitted," she said firmly, but with tears in her eyes, to the official who brought the good news. "I knew it."

Fashionable President Arthur, who lived luxuriously in the mansion during his one term in the 1880's, showed another side of his nature when he was alone. Like Jackson, he too was a recent widower and, like

President Bush walks with Millie and her puppies on the south lawn (opposite). Barbara Bush beams at Margaret and Marvin Bush's new son, Charles Walker (left). Even in the Oval Office (left, below), the President can usually find time for a grandchild. Walker's sister Marshall listens carefully as her grandfather explains something interesting.

the earlier President, Arthur carried on a ritual of remembrance by ordering fresh flowers to be placed daily next to the photograph of his lovely Ellen.

One of the most touching scenes in the history of the great change-overs that have come to this house occurred in Eleanor Roosevelt's study on the second floor, after the death of her husband. Vice President Truman, summoned to the White House, arrived without knowing of the massive stroke that had ended the President's life at Warm Springs, Georgia. He heard the news from Mrs. Roosevelt.

As Truman described the meeting in his memoirs, he asked Mrs. Roosevelt, "Is there anything I can do for you?"

He would never forget her reply, he wrote. "Is there anything *we* can do for *you?*" she said. "For you are the one in trouble now."

Grief, both national and personal, has been too frequent a caller at the President's House. Eight Chief Executives have died in office, four of them by assassination.

Unlike the murders of Lincoln and Garfield, the third slaying was committed far from Washington. In September 1901 McKinley was shaking hands with visitors at the Pan American Exposition in Buffalo,

New York, when a young man extended his left hand to the President, then shot him with a concealed revolver. The attack, by an anarchist named Leon Czolgosz, mortally wounded the President. McKinley died eight days later. The courage and strength in adversity of his widow, Ida, would amaze all who had known her as an almost helpless invalid.

Sixty-two years later, another assassin pressed a trigger in Dallas. As waves of shock spread from that Texas city, President John F. Kennedy lay dead in the prime of life. Then, once more, the casket of a Chief Executive rested in the black-draped East Room of the White House. From all over the globe came an extraordinary procession of the world's great—heads of state, prime ministers, and royalty—to pay their last respects and to share the grief of Kennedy's family and friends.

Y ET WHATEVER FATE befalls the President, the Presidency never dies. Perhaps that is why Americans never tire of stories about the men who have held this office. And why millions turned on their television sets to follow the White House tours conducted by President Truman after the building's reconstruction, by Jacqueline Kennedy when she showed off antiques acquired through her special historical project, and by Tricia Nixon when she took her audience through family rooms on the second floor in 1970. In September 1989, President and Mrs. Bush gave television viewers another personal tour of the second-floor family quarters, including the Lincoln Bedroom, the President's Office, and rare views from the Truman Balcony.

In 1959, Mrs. Eisenhower led an unusual tour of the White House. Her guests were all children or descendants of former Presidents, beginning with John Adams. Eight were sons and daughters of Chief Executives from Cleveland to Eisenhower. History traveled with the party as past residents of the house moved upstairs and down, swapping

In the East Room President and Mrs. Bush, Hollywood stars, local choral groups, and leaders of literacy programs from across the United States welcome the eight recipients of the 1990 National Literacy Honors: three teachers, two national figures, and three "new learners"—adults whose newly gained literacy skills have meant success for themselves and for others.

anecdotes about how it was when they knew "life with father" here.

Alice Roosevelt Longworth recalled the three circular Victorian otto-mans, crowned by potted palms, that once stood in the East Room: ". . . the tops in the center came off," she said, "and my brothers and sister would hide there." Eleanor Wilson McAdoo wanted to quash the myth that pictured her father as "an intellectual snob" and "a grim old Presbyterian." In fact, she said, he was "our most amusing and gay companion."

A note of sadness crept into the nostalgia when the group came to the Lincoln Bedroom, which had been the room that John Coolidge shared with his younger brother, Calvin. Calvin, Jr., then barely 16, died in the summer of 1924—the result of blood poisoning that had developed after he rubbed a blister on his toe while playing tennis on the south grounds. "When he went," his father wrote in his autobiography, "the power and glory of the Presidency went with him."

All of the home-comers agreed that Mrs. Eisenhower's choice of col-ors had brightened the often somber family apartment. And all but one received a surprise when the group made its way down the center hall to the President's Office. At that time it was called the Monroe Room be-cause it contained copies of President Monroe's furniture, including a replica of the desk on which he signed his famous Doctrine.

Pausing before this desk, Laurence Gouverneur Hoes, Monroe's great-great-grandson, pressed a panel that opened to reveal a secret compartment even Mrs. Eisenhower had not known about. Such a com-partment, it turned out, had been discovered in the original desk in 1906, and young Hoes had been indirectly responsible for the find. As a small boy, he had somehow damaged this treasured family possession, and its repair had disclosed the hidden space. In it lay priceless letters written by Jefferson, Madison, Marshall, and Lafayette.

On May 6, 1990, White House portraits provide a backdrop as President Bush greets the East Room audience for biographer David McCullough's talk about Theodore Roosevelt. This program, the second in the Presidential Lecture Series on the Presidency, was telecast later on PBS stations.

4

A HOUSE
FOR THE AGES

HE WAS THE PRESIDENT of the United States. He stood at the pinnacle of a political man's career. Yet he entered the White House without his wife and recently bereft of his only child to survive infancy; and on his inauguration night he slept in a house that was in utter disarray.

Such was the plight of Franklin Pierce on March 4, 1853. His personal life was filled with tragedy and bitterness; his wife had opposed his running for the Presidency, and she interpreted the death of their 11-year-old son Benjamin in a railway accident as a sacrifice demanded by God to leave her husband free to meet his national responsibilities. Mrs. Pierce did not arrive at the White House until later that month.

On the morning of what should have been his most triumphant day, President-elect Pierce had been escorted to the Capitol by the outgoing Chief Executive, Millard Fillmore. He delivered his inaugural address before a cheering crowd and rode to the White House, where for hours he accepted the congratulations of well-wishers.

It was growing late when the last of the handshakers departed, leaving behind soiled dishes and disarranged furniture. The servants had disappeared, and President Pierce and his private secretary, Sidney Webster, groped their way upstairs by candlelight to get what sleep they could before facing the problems of the new administration.

The chaotic conditions that met Franklin Pierce seem incredible now

Streamers of light etch the sky above the White House, lending color to drifts of smoke. The fireworks cannonade, synchronized to the music of Tchaikovsky's 1812 Overture, ended a picnic given for Members of Congress in May 1978.

in comparison with the smooth operation of the modern Executive Mansion. In Pierce's time, Presidents were expected to make their own living arrangements and to provide their own household help and supplies. Indeed, until the early 20th century the President had to pay for all of his and his family's daily needs, whether personal or in connection with official duties. He provided his own horses and carriages and was responsible for their upkeep.

To be sure, Congress appropriated money for repairs and furnishings for the mansion. To many people the annual Presidential salary of $25,000 seemed enough to take care of everything else. But the appropriations often varied with the whims of Congress, and the cost of maintaining a household that reflected the dignity of the nation worked a hardship on many Presidents. Jefferson and Monroe later were forced to sell land to pay debts accumulated during their White House years.

Jefferson's numerous and lavish gourmet dinners—the result of a habit he acquired in France of "mitigating business with dinner"—virtually ate up his salary. In eight years his bills for wine alone came to nearly $11,000. And he once noted that when Congress was in session he needed a great deal more wine, especially champagne. Washington food costs were higher, too, than elsewhere. Jefferson's grocery bill often amounted to $50 a day—at a time when 75 cents for a turkey and $3 for a hog were considered high prices.

It was not until the Taft Administration that Congress relieved Presidents of having to pay the wages of house servants. Harding was the first President for whom the government picked up the check for official entertaining.

Congress also has recognized the advancing level of salaries in the United States, though the sums paid the Chief Executive have lagged behind those received by many corporation presidents. In 1873, effective with Grant's second term, Congress raised the President's salary from $25,000 a year to $50,000. Taft, in 1909, became the first Chief Executive to earn $75,000; Truman, in 1949, was the first to receive $100,000. Since 1969, the annual salary has been $200,000.

The President, however, still must defray the First Family's living expenses. He pays for their food, laundry, and dry cleaning, for their personal telephone calls, and for all their private parties. Ford, for example, paid for a Thanksgiving brunch he gave at the White House to celebrate the 44th reunion of his high-school football team from Grand Rapids.

President Carter footed the bill for daughter Amy's party on her tenth birthday, October 19, 1977. She invited 14 guests, mostly friends from the Thaddeus Stevens School. Planned by Amy and her mother in keeping with the Halloween season, the partygoers watched the original Frankenstein movie. Similarly, whenever one of his grandchildren celebrates a birthday at the White House, or when he and Barbara

President Franklin Pierce, candle in hand, leads his secretary upstairs in a dark, disordered White House after his inaugural reception in 1853. A troubled term followed this disheartening beginning.

give parties for family or friends, President Bush picks up the tab.

Unlike President Pierce, the Chief Executive and First Lady who arrive at the White House today find a trained permanent staff ready to help manage what has now become a highly complex organization.

In many ways the house resembles a small, well-run hotel. Bed and table linens, glasses, silverware, and china—state and informal—are all provided. A storekeeper takes care of the daily marketing needs, and the Secret Service checks the purchases before delivery.

Back in William Henry Harrison's day, White House life was so casual that the President sometimes did his own marketing, carrying his groceries home in a basket. Mrs. Taft hired the first housekeeper in 1909, to supervise the food buying and the preparation of meals for both the President's family and guests. Previously a steward had seen to routine marketing, and caterers met special requirements.

Each incoming First Lady may make selections from furniture already in the mansion or from a government storehouse containing pieces used by previous tenants. And, of course, she may refurnish and redecorate the second- and third-floor quarters as she chooses. The Ground Floor Corridor and principal public rooms on the first floor, however, will retain their museum character, in accordance with a law passed by Congress in 1961 to protect and continue the historical restoration begun by Mrs. Kennedy. Any proposed changes or additions in these rooms must now be approved by the Committee for the Preservation of the White House, established in 1964 by Executive Order.

Workmen hang a chandelier in the restored East Room during the 1948-52 reconstruction of the White House under President Harry Truman.

In recent decades the President's wife has needed increasing help to keep her house presentable for the functions held there for the many and varied groups she is expected to entertain, and for the hundreds of thousands of visitors who tour the mansion.

The combined domestic and maintenance staffs—most of whom carry on from one administration to another—number about 100 employees: maids, laundresses, cooks, butlers, carpenters, painters, engineers, and plumbers. At the head of these workers stands the Chief Usher; his job of coordinating the manifold activities covers just about everything but ushering. If such a force seems large, consider how prodigious are the tasks, and how great the responsibility that goes with handling some of the nation's most valuable possessions. Consider, too, the normal wear and tear involved, and the cleaning, dusting, mopping, and polishing needed after some 35,000 sightseers pass through the state rooms in a single week of the peak tourist season.

The big kitchens opening off the arched Ground Floor Corridor are any chef's dream of equipment and working space. In this gleaming

In the second-floor President's Dining Room (right), David and Julie Nixon Eisenhower join her parents and sister, Tricia, for dinner. An 18th-century chandelier highlights the wallpaper, "The War of Independence." The first-floor Family Dining Room (below, as it looked in the 1890's) serves now chiefly for special occasions.

HARPER'S NEW MONTHLY MAGAZINE (BELOW); WHITE HOUSE PHOTOGRAPH

white and stainless-steel domain stand grinders, slicers, choppers, mixers, coffee roasters, electric ovens, and walk-in freezers. They help Executive Chef Hans Raffert and assistants prepare state dinners for as many as 140 guests, and hors d'oeuvres for 1,000 or more.

Such expert aid would have appeared nothing short of miraculous to those excellent housekeepers Abigail Adams and Dolley Madison. Mrs. Adams wrote to her sister that she would have been pleased just to have had enough candles "lighting the apartments, from the kitchen to parlors and chambers . . . [and] wood enough to keep fires." Mrs. Madison

"superintended all her domestic arrangements before breakfast," one of her biographers noted.

According to an admiring woman correspondent in the 1860's, a morning chore performed by capable Martha Patterson, daughter of President Andrew Johnson, was to "don a calico dress and spotless apron, and then descend to skim the milk and attend the dairy."

As recently as the Taft Administration, a cow named Pauline Wayne supplied milk for the household and grazed on the White House lawn.

Through the years, accounts of the latest home conveniences and

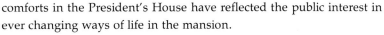

In the gleaming White House kitchen, Nancy Reagan samples dishes prepared by Roland Mesnier (left), pastry chef; Henry Haller, chief chef (center); and cook Frank Ruta. Mrs. Reagan consults with the chefs before special events, offering suggestions for imaginative desserts such as the spun-sugar elephant and swan creations on the table. Below, pots, pans, and pitchers line open shelves in the White House family kitchen of 1890.

comforts in the President's House have reflected the public interest in ever changing ways of life in the mansion.

The building Jefferson moved into in 1801 may have been "big enough for two emperors, one pope, and the grand lama," as a satirist observed, but it lacked practical arrangements for the everyday management of a home. So the President added colonnaded wings on either side of the mansion; they contained servants' quarters, workshops, an icehouse, a meat house, a wine cellar, and a hen house. Inside, the inventive Mr. Jefferson devised a series of revolving trays, called dumbwaiters, which he had built into the walls of his dining room, now the Family Dining Room. With this contrivance, guests could be served from outside the room without having waiters close enough to overhear private conversations. "You need not speak so low," Jefferson once assured a nervous guest. "Our walls have no ears."

Probably the greatest inconvenience of the early White House was the lack of running water. In the few months John and Abigail Adams lived there, servants had to haul water from nearly half a mile away. Jefferson set up an attic cistern with a system of wooden pipes reaching through the floors. But it was not until 1833, in Jackson's second term, that a system of iron pipes brought in spring water and permitted the old frontiersman to enjoy hot and cold showers.

Van Buren put in a basement "reservoir" with a "double-forcing pump" to supply water for kitchen and bathing needs. He thereby added fuel to the political fires stoked by Congressman Charles Ogle. In the "Gold Spoon" speech that accused the President of dining in decadent luxury, Ogle ridiculed him as one who indulged in the Grecian and Roman "pleasures of the warm or tepid bath. . . ." The precise date of the introduction of modern plumbing in the White House remains in doubt. But records show that in 1853 the family quarters had bathtubs with hot and cold running water. By 1876, water to several tubs and water closets was supplied by pipes connected to a 2,000-gallon tank in the attic.

The chronology of other improvements is clearer. In December 1848 the Polks became the first Presidential couple to exchange oil lamps and candlelight for gas illumination. At a reception given soon after, the "brilliant jets suddenly vanished," leaving the guests in darkness—except in the East Room. There, Mrs. Polk said with satisfaction, she had had the foresight to retain the "elegant chandelier," whose "wax candles were shedding their soft radiance." President and Mrs. Fillmore introduced a kitchen stove in the 1850's, a newfangled contraption for the cook who had been preparing even the most lavish meals at a big, open fireplace filled with kettles, pots, skillets, hooks, and cranes.

From the start, the big rooms have been hard to heat. "Hell itself couldn't warm that corner," Jackson complained. The first central furnace—a coal-fueled, hot-water and hot-air system—was installed in 1853, after Franklin Pierce moved in.

President and Mrs. Benjamin Harrison introduced electric lighting but were timid about using it. Ike Hoover, who became Chief Usher

A wide variety of people have always been needed to keep the White House operating. At top, Archie Roosevelt salutes as brother Quentin stands at ease during a roll call of the White House police. Bottom, from left to right: In the late 1800's, a houseman wields a feather duster; at the turn of the century, a messenger makes a delivery on horseback; today, volunteers help decorate the state rooms for Christmas.

during the Taft Administration, began his 42-year White House career in 1891 by setting up the novel system. He wrote later that the Harrisons "were afraid to turn the lights on and off for fear of getting a shock."

As each renovation and improvement brought in more wires, pipes, and flues, walls and structural supports reflected the strain on the old house. The weird tappings and creakings that had bred ghost stories for years finally forced an engineering survey in 1948. The report disclosed that the structure "was standing up," as one investigator put it, "purely from habit." The alternatives: Reconstruct it or tear it down.

Backed by public pleas to save the White House, Congress provided funds to rip out the interior and restore it within the original shell. When the work was completed in 1952, the house at last was "built for ages to come," as Abigail Adams had seen it in 1800. It also was supplied with comforts that would have startled President Fillmore, who called it his "temple of inconveniences."

The big attic where Lincoln's and Theodore Roosevelt's children had played was transformed into a spacious bedroom annex for visiting friends and family. The Coolidges' "Sky Parlor," with its magnificent view to the south, became a solarium. Presidents and their wives, from the Eisenhowers on, have found this bright room a pleasant spot for informal entertaining, or a place to relax and read, to listen to records, or to watch television. The Carter family used the Solarium as a kind of second living room, more casual than the second-floor sitting halls.

Children and adolescents have turned the room into a busy and happy place. Here was the Kennedy kindergarten; here Luci Johnson, surrounded by furniture she had painted, had her teenage hideaway; and here Susan Ford exchanged news and confidences with her brothers.

In their turn, George and Barbara Bush have made use of this sun-flooded room, with its many windows and its muted floral colors. Like Rosalynn Carter and Nancy Reagan, Mrs. Bush has held private luncheons for personal friends in the Solarium.

Work on the White House is never truly finished. During the Carter years, renovation of the exterior began. The removal of some 27 coats of paint, repairing the stone, and repainting will go on until 1992. During the Reagan tenure, the security system was improved, and a special visitors' entrance was added. Outside this entrance, East Executive Avenue has been transformed into a tree-lined pedestrian mall.

Of all the additions to the mansion's facilities, probably the most useful was the second-floor dining room, with its pantry and kitchen. It was converted from a bedroom suite by Mrs. Kennedy to permit the family to have meals served in the private quarters.

In this, the President's Dining Room, as it has been officially named, the Bush family eats their meals together, and from time to time luncheons and dinners are arranged for special guests. A week after they moved into the White House, George and Barbara Bush gave an official dinner in the upstairs dining room—to honor U.N. Secretary General Javier Perez de Cuellar and his wife, Marcela. The Bushes have since held

Workmen rebuild the interior of the White House on a framework of steel beams erected within the original shell. The complete renovation began in 1948, when President Truman noticed chandeliers swaying ominously. He ordered a study of the mansion, and a commission found it so weakened by years of alterations that the Trumans immediately moved across Pennsylvania Avenue to historic Blair House.

many small dinners there with guests ranging from sports stars to journalists, Members of Congress, and personal friends. At these gatherings, President and Mrs. Bush can meet and socialize with their guests in a relaxed and intimate way, which they enjoy doing. The many important visitors that the Bushes have entertained in the President's Dining Room include Queen Elizabeth II and Prince Philip of Great Britain, who had lunch there in May 1991.

Mrs. Bush often entertains personal guests in the Presidential Dining Room. In May 1989 she gave a luncheon there for old friends from the days when George Bush was a Representative from Texas. She also uses the room occasionally for gatherings that spotlight her many programs to further literacy and other causes.

The President's Dining Room itself serves as a display case for such antiques in the White House Collection as a Sheraton pedestal table, Sheraton chairs, and a New England sideboard that belonged to Daniel

As the renovation nears completion, carpenters (upper left) hang doors, and movers lug in furniture. Artisans (above) attach original moldings to a fireplace pillar. The Trumans moved back from Blair House in March 1952 after four years of work that cost $5,761,000.

Webster. The blue-tone wallpaper depicts scenes of the American Revolution based on engravings of the early 19th century. Studying the wallpaper during a small dinner in May 1981, Great Britain's Prince Charles good-naturedly chided President Reagan for seating him so that all evening he had to look at Lord Cornwallis's surrender at Yorktown.

This same wallpaper was part of the Kennedy decor in 1961 and lasted through the Johnson and Nixon periods. Mrs. Ford had the paper removed and the walls painted a solid "sunny yellow." The Carters rehung the Revolutionary scenes, which had been preserved for possible future use, and the historic wallpaper remains there today.

It is all part of the continuous change that goes on in and around this house. At one Nixon dinner party in the upstairs dining room, Alice Roosevelt Longworth surprised and amused her hosts and other guests when she suddenly exclaimed, "My goodness . . . this is the room where I had my appendix out."

5

IN THE
PRESIDENT'S PARK

UNDER A CLOUDLESS BLUE SKY the Prime Minister's limousine rolled along the south lawn driveway to the White House. It was March 21, 1990, and Prime Minister Tadeusz Mazowiecki of the Republic of Poland was making an official call on the President of the United States. The audience waited expectantly, each group in its assigned place: leading U. S. officials; a representative of the Diplomatic Corps; reporters; a battery of video and still photographers on their platform; and the public, admitted for the event.

As the Prime Minister and his party reached the Southwest Gate, President and Mrs. Bush emerged from the Diplomatic Reception Room. The U. S. Army Herald Trumpets then played four "Ruffles and Flourishes" followed by "Hail to the Chief." When the visitors arrived at the White House, President and Mrs. Bush came forward to shake hands and to present Vice President and Mrs. Quayle and other officials to them. The President escorted the Prime Minister along the traditional red carpet to the reviewing stand. The U. S. Army Herald Trumpets again played four "Ruffles and Flourishes." As a 19-gun salute was fired, the U. S. Marine Band played the Polish national anthem, followed by the national anthem of the United States.

The Third U. S. Infantry, the historic Old Guard Fife and Drum Corps, trooped in review on the broad expanse of the south lawn. Then

Screened by greenery, the Rose Garden provides privacy for outdoor activities of the Presidential families. Barbara Bush relaxes here amid flowering fruit trees with her English springer spaniel Millie, and one of Millie's puppies.

President Bush officially welcomed the Prime Minister. He responded with a speech that reflected the ties of the two friendly countries. Thus another foreign leader—Prime Minister of a nation that has recently emerged as a young democracy and begun warm diplomatic relations with the United States—had begun an official visit. The leading figures in the opening pageant could now attend a brief reception in the mansion and get on to problems of international concern.

THIS WELCOMING CEREMONY was first introduced by President Kennedy, and it has remained largely unchanged. In his time, it also included helicopter service to transport guests to the arrival rites. Johnson, Nixon, Ford, and Carter maintained the lift, though less frequently, but the practice has now come into disuse. Most state guests arrive the day before and are driven through the Southwest Gate to the meeting the next morning.

Helicopters, however, have become an important feature of Presidential travel. Eisenhower was first to use them for trips to and from the White House. The choppers have continued to touch down on a pad near the south entrance. They lift Presidents to nearby airfields, bring consultants to the mansion, and fly First Families to the Maryland retreat named Camp David for Eisenhower's grandson.

Both the helicopter flights and the state arrival ceremony, with its spectacular sound and color, have taken their place in the succession of historic acts presented on this outdoor stage for nearly two centuries.

Jefferson's Fourth of July celebrations included reviews of the District militia and other troops in the newly laid out "President's Park," with "their gay appearance and martial musick," wrote an eyewitness, "enlivening the scene, exhilerating the spirits of the throngs of people who poured in from the country and adjacent towns."

On April 10, 1865, jubilant crowds surged across the White House lawns, singing and cheering over the news of Gen. Robert E. Lee's surrender at Appomattox. Soon President Lincoln came to a window in response to the cries of the people. He promised them he would make a victory speech later, but meantime he suggested that their enthusiastic band play "Dixie." It was one of the best tunes he had ever heard, he said, and he thought "we had fairly captured it."

When the Air Age was young in 1911, the broad south grounds of the White House witnessed a prophetic and dramatic sight. A pioneering pilot, Harry Nelson Atwood, landed there in a Burgess-Wright biplane soon after completing a record-setting cross-country flight, and President Taft presented him with a gold medal for the feat.

Over the years, the 18-acre estate that today surrounds the White House with well-kept gardens and lawns has shown different faces. John and Abigail Adams found it a barren expanse littered with workmen's shacks and tools. The grounds had appeared so grim before their arrival, in fact, that a member of the President's Cabinet wrote to one of the District Commissioners complaining that "a private gentleman pre-

"A most fitting addition to the White House," commented Leslie's *in 1858 on Buchanan's new conservatory. The President's niece Harriet Lane walked here among her camellias to escape "the constant whirl of fashion." On public days visitors marveled at South American orange trees, aloes, and pitcher plants.*

FRANK LESLIE'S ILLUSTRATED NEWSPAPER, TINTED BY P. HALL BAGLIE

paring a residence for his Friend, would have done more than has been done." He suggested that the Commissioners plant "something like a garden, at the North side of . . . [the] large, naked, ugly looking building. . . ." and provide a yard enclosure.

But it was President Jefferson who obtained funds to build the first fence. For a few years, this rustic rail-and-post enclosure blended nicely into a village Capital where "Excellent snipe shooting and even partridge shooting was to be had on either side of the main avenue. . . ," as the secretary of the British Legation noted. Then Jefferson replaced the wood fence with a fieldstone wall and constructed an imposing arched gate over the driveway leading to the North Entrance.

With his architect Benjamin Latrobe, Jefferson also devised an overall landscape plan. It included grading and planting the south grounds to provide more privacy, while leaving a central view toward the river.

It remained, however, for that austere New Englander and ardent gardener, John Quincy Adams, to devote the most lavish personal care of any President to the White House nurseries and gardens.

In his diaries from 1825 to 1829 appear entries that tell of the happy hours he spent on this hobby. The accounts reveal his enjoyment of pungent herbs—balm, rue, sage, tansy, and tarragon—and his delight in the "deep blood-colored beet, the white-flowered carrot and yellow-flowered parsnip. . . ."

In this "small garden, of less than two acres. . . ," he wrote, there were "forest- and fruit-trees, shrubs, hedges, esculent vegetables, kitchen and medicinal herbs, hot-house plants, flowers and weeds, to the amount, I conjecture, of at least one thousand."

As had Jefferson, Adams planned to introduce useful crops to American farmers. On his rides about Washington and on travels to and from his Massachusetts home, he collected nuts, seeds, and seedlings, and encouraged his friends to do the same when they went abroad.

After Congress passed a resolution to encourage the growing of mulberry trees to form a base for a silkworm industry in the United States, Adams added the white mulberry to his flourishing White House nurseries. With his wife Louisa, he nurtured silkworms on the leaves, and in the evenings he would sit beside her, writing, as she unreeled and rewound the fragile silk filaments from the cocoons.

Adams's dream of a silk industry never materialized. But one of his shade trees remains—a great American elm that spreads its branches over the southeast lawn.

WITH THE ARRIVAL of Andrew Jackson and the building of the North Portico that completed construction of the mansion, the evolution of the grounds entered a new phase. Instead of the rambling gardens of Adams, graveled footways appeared, along with a carriage house, driveway, and stable for the President's favorite racing horses. More lasting than either carriages or stable would be another Jackson innovation—a magnificent magnolia, in memory of his beloved Rachel, that still stands beside the South Portico.

As Washington grew less bucolic, the President's Park was enhanced with fountains and flower beds. In 1841, when Dickens called to see President Tyler, he found the "ornamental ground about it . . . laid out in garden walks; they are pretty and agreeable to the eye; though they have that uncomfortable air of having been made yesterday. . . ."

Time and professional landscape architects, including the talented Andrew Jackson Downing, would overcome the effect of newness that Dickens observed. Within 15 years, the White House estate, particularly its tree-dotted south lawn, had become part of "a scene of beauty and attractiveness. . . ," according to an article in an 1856 issue of *United States Magazine*. Open to the public on weekdays, the "agreeable promenades" drew "the élite of the city," said the author. "Usually the President, the Cabinet, and the Foreign Ministers and their wives may be seen here [with] thousands of ladies and pretty children, most bewitchingly dressed. . . ."

Around this time, President Buchanan's niece and official hostess, Harriet Lane, persuaded her uncle to build one of the greenhouses that would give much pleasure to future White House residents and visitors.

Stern-faced soldier for women's rights holds aloft her banner at the northwest corner of the White House grounds. During the Wilson Administration, before the Nineteenth Amendment gave women the vote, suffragettes picketed the White House, went on hunger strikes, and got themselves jailed. The President called their methods "unfortunate."

LIBRARY OF CONGRESS, CA 1917

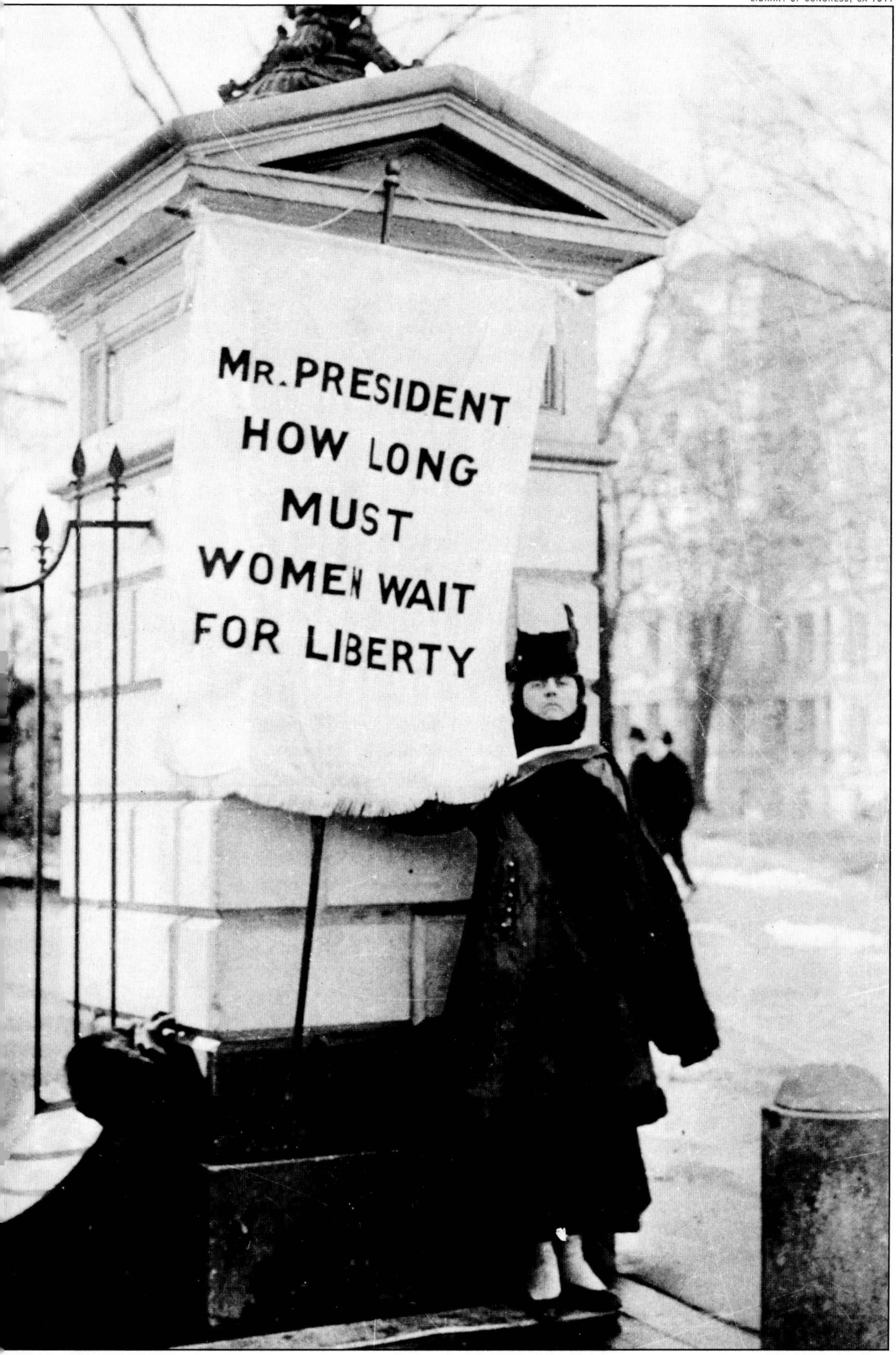

Lucy Hayes worked there with trowel and shears among her lilies and roses. Frances Cleveland spent pleasant hours wandering with her girls along the sweet-scented aisles of the greenhouses. Caroline Harrison was fond of orchids—an interest that led to her own orchid-painted china. Out of that interest grew the White House china collection representing almost every Presidential family.

From the time Buchanan's conservatories opened until they were torn down to make way for the West Wing, no First Lady had far to go for flowers or potted plants to decorate her home. Today, gardeners of the Washington area occasionally donate flowers, but most flowers for arrangements come from wholesale distributors. Greenhouses of the National Park Service, which is responsible for the care and upkeep of the mansion and its grounds, supply potted plants.

The floral preferences of First Ladies make a varied bouquet. Mrs. Eisenhower's favorites were sweetheart roses and pink carnations. Mrs. Kennedy experimented with mixed floral designs, and Mrs. Johnson favored variety, from spring pastels to deeper shades of fall. Mrs. Nixon took keen interest in planning floral colors and designs for state dinners. Mrs. Ford showed a definite preference for all kinds of lilies. And Mrs. Carter's choices followed the Kennedy style with simple garden flowers, such as roses and daisies.

The present White House floral designer, Nancy Clarke, follows Mrs. Bush's taste in flowers for the house. An avid gardener, Mrs. Bush is especially fond of peonies, lilies, gardenias, and all varieties of daisies.

The big event in White House decor comes at Christmas, when each First Lady makes the nation's official home beautiful for the season and the public. Mrs. Bush is aided by skilled volunteers who come from all over the country to assist in the decorating. For her first holiday season in the Executive Mansion, Barbara Bush helped trim the official White House Christmas tree, an 18-foot-tall Fraser fir in the Blue Room. Her concern for family literacy provided the theme for the tree. It was decorated with soft-sculpture dolls depicting storybook characters, including Little Red Riding Hood, Mary Poppins, Pinocchio, Oliver Twist, and Babar the Elephant, a Bush family favorite.

The following year, the traditional gingerbread house, baked by the White House Executive Chef, Hans Raffert, had a new Bush touch—a doghouse for Millie, the Bush springer spaniel, with a miniature Millie outside it. *The Nutcracker* ballet provided the theme for the official tree.

Beginning with Woodrow Wilson, all the Presidents, and some of their wives, have planted trees in the President's Park. George Bush has added an ash, a beech, and a linden to the south lawn.

Many Presidents have set up recreational facilities on the grounds. Hayes marked off a croquet court near the South Portico, where, a staff member wrote, clerks as well as the family "used to spend an hour now and then . . . over hard-fought games with mallet and ball." There has been a tennis court on the south lawn since the time of Theodore Roosevelt. The press called associates who joined him for a fast, tough game

For relaxation and fitness, Presidents turn to sports. George Bush pitches horseshoes, as did Harry Truman. Right, Gerald Ford swims a lap for the press.

his "tennis Cabinet." Harding practiced his golf shots on the lawn and trained his Airedale, Laddie Boy, to retrieve the balls. Hoover exercised with his "medicine-ball Cabinet" before breakfast conferences under the magnolias. Truman pitched horseshoes; Eisenhower improved his golf on a Presidential putting green.

Ford installed the first outdoor swimming pool, near the Oval Office. The Carter family enjoyed the pool, the tennis courts, and the bowling alley under the North Portico. President Reagan had no opportunity to enjoy his favorite exercise, horseback riding, on the White House grounds. Both he and the First Lady used exercise equipment installed in a second-floor bedroom, on the recommendation of his doctors after the assassination attempt.

George Bush, a very active President, has installed a horseshoe pit and a basketball half-court. He also jogs, plays golf, and practices golf shots on the grounds. Mrs. Bush plays tennis, swims, and enjoys strolling on the lawn with Millie and the President's dog, Ranger.

C HILDREN PARTICULARLY have found the rolling acres of the south lawn a great playground. Here they can explore hidden nooks in hedges and bushes, ride ponies, and raise pets of every description. Little Tad Lincoln made a pet of a turkey that relatives sent for the family's Christmas dinner in 1863. He named it Jack. When the cook prepared to kill the turkey, Tad ran in tears to his father, who interrupted a Cabinet meeting to write an official reprieve.

Another President's son faced a less amenable father. T. R. once caught young Quentin walking on stilts through a flower bed. The boy obeyed Roosevelt's stern order to get out of the flowers, but grumbled, "I don't see what good it does *me* for you to be President."

Once a year all Washington youngsters are invited to an egg-rolling party on the south grounds. On most Easter Mondays, starting with the Hayes Administration, children have brought baskets of decorated hard-boiled eggs to this party—now one of the last events at the President's House still open to all the public.

The White House Easter Egg Roll of March 27, 1989, was one of the most spectacular in history. Some 30,000 people came—children eight years old or younger, with their required escorts. They found the south lawn a dazzling sight, with helium-filled balloons in pastel shades, clowns, bands, mimes, tumblers, and a petting zoo with farm animals, including chicks and bunnies. Among the celebrities present were the Easter bunny and Christopher Reeve, star of the movie *Superman*.

President Bush, attending with the First Lady and six grandchildren, blew a whistle to start a round of the egg rolling. The object is to see how fast a child can push a hard-boiled egg down a grassy slope with a spoon. All of the participants were winners; each took home as a souvenir one of 23,000 wooden eggs bearing the signature of the President or Mrs. Bush. Younger children hunted for the wooden eggs in straw-covered areas of the park or listened to stories being read aloud.

Racing and tumbling down a hillock, children romp on the south lawn during the 1887 Easter Monday egg rolling. More than a century later, on March 27, 1989, the Bush Easter egg hunt and roll attracted some 30,000 participants. At right, the Easter bunny stops to chat with Pierce and Lauren, children of Neil and Sharon Bush.

Red-coated Old Guard Fife and Drum Corps troops in review on the south lawn during the welcoming ceremony for Poland's Prime Minister Mazowiecki on March 21, 1990. Moments earlier, batteries had fired a 19-gun salute while the Marine Corps Band played the Polish national anthem and then the

"Star-Spangled Banner." The Prime Minister stands next to President Bush on the red-carpeted platform. Name tags on the lawn position guests of honor, including Mrs. Bush and the U. S. Chief of Protocol, to the right of the stand. Other guests (far right) and press members (left) watch from behind rope cordons.

Microphone in hand, President Wilson talks with a pilot circling overhead in a demonstration of air-ground communication on November 22, 1918. Half a century later, on July 21, 1969, television captures an event witnessed by millions across the globe: President Nixon talks by radiotelephone with the first men on the moon—Apollo 11 Astronauts Neil A. Armstrong and Edwin E. Aldrin, Jr.

In 1991, the theme for the Egg Roll was literacy, highlighting Mrs. Bush's interest in furthering family reading. Each child leaving the White House received a canvas bag filled with cookies, and books and magazines to read.

Whatever the event, few settings could be lovelier than the rolling expanse of lawn as viewed from the balcony added to the South Portico during the Truman Administration. Looking past a shimmering pool and fountains toward the Washington Monument and Jefferson Memorial, a visitor today would find it hard to realize that this area once merged with malarial marshes along a creek, which by 1817 had been walled and deepened into a sluggish canal. Odorous with sewage, garbage, and dead animals, alive with mosquitoes and flies, the canal was the bane of White House occupants.

As a summer retreat, Van Buren rented a house in nearby Georgetown. Buchanan and Lincoln were glad to go back and forth in hot months to a cottage lent them at the Soldiers' Home three miles away. "I am alone in the White pest-house," a Lincoln secretary wrote a friend. "The ghosts of twenty thousand drowned cats come in at night through the south windows." In 1872 the canal-sewer was covered and the street it created was named Constitution Avenue. With filling and landscaping, the present Ellipse was completed by 1884. Future Presidents could graciously entertain outdoors.

THE THEODORE ROOSEVELTS started the trend with a series of lawn parties, inviting Cabinet members and other friends. When President and Mrs. Taft celebrated their silver anniversary in June 1911, they received more than 3,000 guests on the south grounds, where trees and bushes sparkled with tiny, colored lights, and strings of paper lanterns cast shadows on the lawn. Mrs. Taft later wrote happily of the occasion that "a more brilliant throng was never gathered in this country." In the summer of 1918 President and Mrs. Wilson began inviting war veterans to attend an annual garden fete.

Summer after summer, the south lawn has offered a perfect setting for large gatherings. The Eisenhowers, for example, held a reception there for more than 4,000 members of the American Bar Association and counselors from the British Commonwealth.

The Kennedy children shared their playground with 1,700 youngsters from child-care agencies when the kilted Black Watch—the Royal Highland Regiment—paraded to the skirl of bagpipes.

On a huge stage erected on the south lawn, President Johnson presented awards to outstanding high-school graduates who had won a place in his annual Presidential-Scholar program, begun in 1964.

In a Rose Garden reception on September 24, 1981, President Reagan honored Sandra Day O'Connor—the first woman to be named to the U. S. Supreme Court. And in April 1983, Reagan presented awards there to outstanding Peace Corps volunteers for using their "God-given talents" in helping others overseas.

President and Mrs. Bush, like their predecessors, make good use of the historic park. The President has held press conferences, signed legislation, presented awards, and saluted winning athletic teams in the Rose Garden. It was there that the President congratulated the Cincinnati Reds after they won the 1990 World Series.

Sometimes it is the President who is honored. On May 14, 1991, during her official visit to the United States, Great Britain's Queen Elizabeth II used the Rose Garden for her presentation of the Winston Churchill Award to President Bush "in recognition of the leadership you have showed to the world in recent months." On a lighter note, on the same visit, the Queen was taken to see the White House horseshoe pit outside the Oval Office. There she gave the President a more personal gift—a set of four silver-plated horseshoes engraved "E II R," for Elizabeth Regina the Second.

Each year the President also accepts a Thanksgiving turkey, presented by the National Turkey Federation, in the Rose Garden. In recent years, the birds have evaded the roasting pan to live out their days as a tourist attraction at a nearby farm park.

The Rose Garden was the setting for dramatic announcements during the Persian Gulf War against Iraq. On March 1, 1991, after heavy bombing of Iraq by the United States and its United Nations allies, President Bush stood there and issued an ultimatum to Iraqi dictator Saddam Hussein. He told Saddam to begin an "immediate and unconditional withdrawal from Kuwait" to avoid a massive ground war offensive by the allied troops.

O N THE SOUTH LAWN, other gatherings and receptions come and go in colorful procession. In April 1989, a picnic was held to dedicate President Bush's new horseshoe pit. Among the many guests invited were players from the Washington Redskins football team, governors, Cabinet Members, business executives, and journalists, including veteran newsman Walter Cronkite. The guests enjoyed an afternoon of hot dogs, hamburgers, and horseshoes with the President.

The tradition of an annual picnic for Members of Congress, held each year on the south lawn, has been kept up by George and Barbara Bush. At the June 1991 picnic, some 500 guests—members of the House and Senate and others—were treated to a New England-style clambake that included whole Maine lobsters, corn on the cob, and ice cream.

After dinner, the country and western band Alabama performed. The President, who enjoys country music, compared his own cowboy boots with those of the lead singer. He then expressed his gratitude for a chance to spend a relaxed evening with the legislators after hard debate and differences with them on the Hill.

"It's wonderful," remarked the President, "nobody moving . . . or seconding the motion. And I've enjoyed it." It was, said the President, a night to "lay aside the politics" and "just have fun."

The President's Park is a wonderful place for children. Above, white-frocked girls dance around a maypole during Hoover's tenure. Right, cedar boughs shade Amy Carter's tree house, also a favorite perch for her nephew Jason. Below, birthday girl, five-year-old Marshall Bush (center, with red bow) smiles as Ranger carefully observes the clown. Among the guests is cousin Ellie LeBlond, in red glasses at right.

6

THE
LONELIEST PLACE...

"NO EASY MATTER will ever come to you...," said President Eisenhower to President-elect Kennedy on the eve of the 1961 inauguration. "If they're easy they will be settled at a lower level."

President Taft called the White House "the loneliest place in the world." After one year in office, Theodore Roosevelt wrote: "Everyday, almost every hour, I have to decide very big as well as very little questions, and ... what it is possible ... to achieve." On President Truman's desk stood a sign that read "The buck stops here." And on the brink of war with Iraq in 1990, President Bush agreed with Truman: "The buck stops there [indicating his desk], and I'll do what I have to do."

As the representative of all the people, the President must balance the often-conflicting interests of many groups and sections in seeking the common good. Yet he can never forget that the individual American also looks directly to him as the holder of the office that—in Herbert Hoover's words—"touches the happiness of every home."

Seldom, if ever, can the Chief Executive escape the pressures of his job, whether engaging in a favorite sport or relaxing in the intimacy of his family circle. To all, friends or strangers, he has suddenly become a man whose magic words can unlock the gifts of position and wealth. His election has given him powers that in scope and variety are unique. He is at once the ceremonial head of government, leader of a political

Unrelenting paperwork keeps outdoorsman Theodore Roosevelt at his desk. He later wrote of "the incredible amount of administrative work with which the President has to deal even in time of peace. He is of necessity a very busy man."

CENTURY MAGAZINE, MARCH 1897 (BELOW); JUDGE, MARCH 23, 1889, BOTH LIBRARY OF CONGRESS

party, administrator of the nation's laws and domestic affairs, director of foreign policy, and Commander in Chief of the Armed Forces.

How this many-faceted power has been used has depended on the era, the character, and the conscience of each President, for the Constitution laid out few specific guidelines for the conduct of the office. As Woodrow Wilson put it, the President is "at liberty . . . to be as big a man as he can. His capacity will set the limit. . . ."

In 1800, when the country was young and weak, John Adams took the initiative in ending an undeclared naval war with France over the sensitive issue of freedom of the seas for United States shipping.

The war then raging between France and Great Britain had led French privateers to seize American merchantmen, and open hostilities broke out. Adams, who at first had been as belligerent as many of his countrymen, turned to efforts at conciliation. When he learned that France was ready to discuss terms, he defied opposition and sent negotiators to Paris, and was so proud of their success that he once suggested having his tombstone record his part in making peace.

Madison faced a far more painful decision in the War of 1812—called "Madison's War" by his foes. Again the quarrel was over freedom of the seas during a war between England and France. But this time Napoleon pretended to respect the United States' neutrality, thus intensifying the outcries against the British for preying on American ships.

Swayed by that fact, and prodded by the "War Hawks" of the West who dreamed of annexing Canada, Madison pressed Congress for a declaration of war against Britain. But at the darkest hour of the conflict, when Dolley Madison and the Cabinet were in flight from the burning Capital, the President must have wondered if he had endangered all that the Revolution had won.

The conclusion of the War of 1812 permitted the nation to look westward again. Surprisingly, the greatest territorial expansion after the Louisiana Purchase was gained by a President seldom mentioned today. In 1844 James K. Polk was a dark-horse candidate, yet he became a strong leader whose policies fixed the western border of the United States along the shores of the Pacific Ocean.

As a follower and protégé of Jackson, Polk was well nicknamed "Young Hickory." Elected as a frank expansionist, he succeeded in bringing most of the present-day Southwest into the Union—though at the cost of an unpopular war with Mexico—and in acquiring the Oregon country north to the 49th parallel by a compromise with Britain. Still quoted today is the catchy slogan, "54-40 or fight," used by Polk's militant followers in demanding the northernmost boundary of the Oregon territory. Yet Polk's own shrewd diplomatic maneuvers that averted a third war with Great Britain have generally been forgotten.

When formulating and promoting policies, most Presidents have shown a high regard for the people's support and understanding.

"I shall go just so fast and only so fast as I think I'm right and the people are ready for the step," said Lincoln. Benjamin Harrison declared

Outgoing President Grover Cleveland leaves successor Benjamin Harrison holding the door in a cartoon deriding the seemingly endless flow of office seekers demanding the Chief Executive's time. At left, applications and recommendations cover the desk as Cleveland and Postmaster General William Lyne Wilson work far into the night appointing postmasters.

that public opinion was "the most potent monarch this world knows."

Indeed, public opinion often may weigh more heavily in a President's decision than advice from his Cabinet. Chief Executives have varied sharply in consulting Cabinet members on important matters—a choice left open by the Constitution. Monroe conferred at length with his Cabinet, and especially with Secretary of State John Quincy Adams, before pronouncing the Monroe Doctrine that warned European powers against further expansion in the Western Hemisphere.

On the other hand, Jackson largely bypassed his Cabinet, preferring to discuss issues with friends, who were disparaged as his "kitchen Cabinet" but who served him capably and loyally.

Even during the first and second World Wars, Presidents Wilson and Roosevelt seldom called a Cabinet session. Roosevelt, like Jackson, chose to confer with outsiders of differing views, and with some of his administrative assistants whose qualifications, he said, were "high competence, great physical vigor, and a passion for anonymity."

Fortunately the Chief Executive does not always face world-shaking decisions. His day-to-day duties, however, are with him always, and have steadily increased. John Adams complained that a "peck of troubles in a large bundle of papers . . . comes every day . . . there is no pleasure."

When John Quincy Adams, in turn, took on the Presidency, the growing paperwork was made almost unbearable by his failure to delegate it. To cope with the minutiae, he used shorthand no one else could decipher, and impaired his eyesight and health by writing thousands of words a week in official and personal correspondence. James K. Polk was similarly inclined. "No President who performs his duty faithfully . . .can have any leisure," he declared. "If he entrusts the details . . . to subordinates constant errors will occur. I prefer to supervise the whole operation of the Government myself. . . ."

Edith Wilson, who married the widower President in 1915, assists her husband.

Already, however, this had become impossible. Polk's attempt to do the task put such a strain on his frail constitution that he became ill and died at age 53, a few months after leaving office.

Congress, too, was slow to provide funds for executive help. Most early Presidents called on a relative to act as private secretary, paying salaries from their own pockets. Congress finally voted money to hire one private secretary for President Buchanan, then the Civil War suddenly increased the need.

Lincoln acquired two bright and talented young secretaries, John Hay and John Nicolay. But no one could shield the President from the burdens of a country at war, nor would he permit himself to be sheltered from the avalanche of problems unloaded by officials, generals, war contractors, cranks, wounded soldiers, and tearful wives and mothers.

Most annoying was the clamor of petitioners for public office, often raised by those without qualifications. Lincoln told of a man who asked for a post as a foreign minister and gradually reduced his demands until he was willing to settle for an old pair of pants.

Office seekers, however, had become pests long before Lincoln's Administration. They and their eager sponsors haunted the White House even in the time of John Adams. Jackson openly used the spoils system to reward his supporters. For a time fear stalked the ranks of his opponents in government service; in all, it is estimated, about one-fifth of the entire work force was replaced.

With each change of administration came fresh hordes of office seekers. During William Henry Harrison's tenure, a group of men once barred him from a Cabinet meeting until he accepted their applications.

President after President complained of the persecution and senseless waste of time. Yet it was not until after Garfield's murder by a thwarted job hunter that firm action was taken. In 1883 Congress passed the Pendleton Act, the first major reform law to open the way to competitive examinations as the basis for most federal service.

The nation was coming of age. Such changes in public attitude toward the obligations and rights of the man in the White House reflected the increasing energy, wealth, and population of the country.

Twentieth-century Presidents, supervising the nerve center of action in the West Wing, have found that the pace of their work has grown ever faster with new technology.

Theodore Roosevelt carried out his dynamic foreign and domestic programs in a period when messengers on horseback or bicycle rushed urgent letters and documents between the White House, Congress, and executive departments. Automobiles came in with Taft. Harding was the first President to broadcast a speech by radio, Truman the first to deliver an address from the White House by television. The first airplane assigned to the Chief Executive was a specially built C-54 used once by Franklin Roosevelt, and later by Truman. Jets have been supplied since Eisenhower's time.

WIDE WORLD

President Franklin D. Roosevelt signs the Social Security Act, August 14, 1935.

BACK IN 1877 President Hayes installed a telephone at the mansion after seeing one demonstrated by inventor Alexander Graham Bell. Yet as late as Taft's term only one operator was needed to handle calls. When the operator went to lunch, young Charlie Taft considered it great sport to take over the switchboard. Today 19 telephone operators routinely take an average of 5,000 calls a day—and thousands more at times of national stress.

Gone are the days when Cleveland could write many of his letters and speeches by hand, or when McKinley and his staff of a dozen people could cope with all of the business. Wilson sometimes picked up a letter from a secretary's desk and answered it on his own typewriter. Harding was the first President to hire a professional speech writer.

As the problems have increased and grown more complex, the Presidential staff has come to include secretaries, consultants, and aides at the White House, plus economic, technical, and other advisory groups in the neighboring Executive Office Buildings.

To their regular schedules, Presidents in this century have added travels abroad. T. R. was the first to leave the United States, when he went to Panama in 1906. Wilson pioneered in going to Europe after World War I; F.D.R. was first to visit South America and Hawaii, and he attended the historic World War II conferences at Casablanca, Tehran, and Yalta. Truman went to Germany for the famous Potsdam Conference held just before the war's end.

Since then every Chief Executive has traveled widely. Johnson was the first to fly around the world on state visits. Nixon also circled the globe, and in 1972 he became the first American head of state to visit the People's Republic of China. Ford met with world leaders in Japan, Korea, and Soviet Asia, as well as in many European countries. And Carter matched all previous records when he and, at times, his wife—as his

First official White House fleet of horseless carriages lines up before the garage—the former stable. William Howard Taft in 1909 ordered (from left) a White steamer, a Baker electric, and two Pierce Arrows.

personal representative—traveled to nations in Europe, the Middle East, Africa, Latin America, and the Caribbean.

During his Presidency, Ronald Reagan traveled widely around the world to meet with foreign leaders. In London in 1982, he gave the first address ever made by an American President to both Houses of Parliament. He also traveled to confer with Soviet leader Mikhail Gorbachev twice, once in Geneva in 1985 and again in Reykjavik, Iceland, in 1986.

President Bush made his first foreign trip in February 1989, when he attended the funeral of Emperor Hirohito of Japan. On this trip, he met with officials in Beijing and Seoul to discuss U. S. policy in Asia. Highlights of the President's later travels included several trips to Europe in 1989. At the NATO summit in Brussels in May, he proposed new initiatives on arms-control. In Bonn, he urged a less militarized Europe, stating that "We are nearer our goals of peace and European reconciliation than at any time since the founding of NATO. . . ."

In July, the President made a five-day visit to Poland and Hungary, then attended the NATO economic summit in Paris. There, he saluted the "absolutely amazing" changes he had seen in Poland and Hungary, mentioning the emergence of a multiparty system in Poland and the destruction of the Iron Curtain between Hungary and Austria.

In December, the President met Soviet leader Gorbachev in Malta to discuss further changes sweeping Europe, including the opening of the Berlin Wall in November. In July 1990, he attended the NATO summit in London. The following summer, President Bush traveled to Moscow for a summit meeting with Gorbachev.

NOTHING BETTER ILLUSTRATES the interest in the President's activities than does the news coverage that follows him wherever he goes. Teams of reporters accompany him on travels, check his daily appointments, quiz him on policy at press conferences.

As an institution, the press conference began when President Wilson initiated formal question-and-answer meetings with reporters to explain his programs. It has continued in varied forms, from requiring reporters to submit written queries to the present rapid-fire questioning under television lights. Originally held in the Oval Office, the conferences were moved to the Old Executive Office Building during the Eisenhower Administration. Now they usually occur in the East Room.

Press facilities have come a long way since Theodore Roosevelt first provided space for reporters in his new West Wing, reputedly after taking pity on newsmen shivering at the gates in a winter storm. Further improvements in press accommodations were made in 1970, when the old newsroom was replaced by a press center built over Franklin Roosevelt's swimming pool. It includes a briefing room and two floors of booths for writers and broadcasters.

Though the news media turn a softer light on the President's wife, every First Lady plays an important part in her own way. Back in John Adams's time, critics felt that witty, politically sophisticated Abigail had

Harry Doll, George Augur, Gracie Doll.

Chiefs of the Sioux nation and President Calvin Coolidge.

Callers from many worlds have found hospitality at the White House. In 1874 King Kalakaua of the Sandwich Islands (now Hawaii) visited Ulysses S. Grant. Harding greeted a circus giant and two midget friends, as well as movie stars Dorothy and Lillian Gish, producer D. W. Griffith, and evangelist Billy Sunday. Coolidge's impassive expression rivaled those of Sioux chiefs visiting in 1925. Hoover presented the National Geographic Society's Gold Medal to Amelia Earhart after her solo Atlantic flight. After his talk with Eisenhower, Prince Faisal stepped onto the snowy grounds in his flowing desert robes. Johnson and Hubert Humphrey pause during their stroll on the lawn to greet sightseers at the Southeast Gate. In 1979 Jimmy and Rosalynn Carter welcomed Pope John Paul II, the first Pontiff to meet with a President in the mansion.

President and Mrs. Carter with Pope John Paul II.

Prince Faisal of Saudi Arabia.

President Eisenhower greeting Indian Prime Minister Jawaharlal Nehru.

King David Kalakaua.

Dorothy Gish, David Wark Griffith, Lillian Gish.

Evangelist Billy Sunday.

President Johnson and Vice President Humphrey shaking hands with tourists.

Truman with General de Gaulle.

Diana Hopkins, Winston Churchill.

Hoover and Amelia Earhart.

too much influence on the President. To one of them she was *"her Maj-esty"* and *"Mrs. President."*

Throughout the 19th century most wives avoided a political role, lim-iting themselves to charity and to mild support of such broad issues as temperance and women's suffrage. Dolley Madison helped found and direct a Capital orphanage, and was said to have contributed "$20 and a cow" to it. Sarah Polk worked as the President's private secretary, clipping and summarizing war news and political reports for him. Edith Wilson protected her ill husband by screening his visitors and official papers so persistently that critics called her "Mrs. President," too.

But the first wife of a President to participate actively in national af-fairs was Eleanor Roosevelt. She offered the first press conferences for newswomen, and produced prime news during the sessions. She trav-eled so much on lectures, visits to overseas troops, and as the "eyes and ears" of F.D.R. that her White House code name was "Rover."

Lady Bird Johnson turned out to be another "Woman Doer," to use the title she created to honor outstanding women, including those ac-tive in her own programs to beautify the landscape and to give needy children a preschool boost to education through "Head Start." Patricia Nixon became a goodwill ambassador to Latin America in 1970. After an earthquake shook a vast area of Peru, she flew into the devastated re-gion in a cargo plane carrying emergency supplies.

Betty Ford, with her personal warmth and interest in people, made friends for her husband and for her country as she traveled with him on trips at home and abroad. Rosalynn Carter embarked on many far-reaching programs, including a national drive that she initiated and led to improve the care of America's mentally ill. Nancy Reagan worked hard to fight drug abuse among children and held conferences at the White House to support drives to combat the problem.

"The war . . . is coming very close to home," F.D.R. warns in a radio broadcast on May 27, 1941, less than seven months before the Japanese attack on Pearl Harbor. The President invited representatives of 20 American republics and Canada to hear his address in the East Room.

While Barbara Bush is actively involved in a number of social service programs, since 1980 her primary focus has been to promote literacy in America. Believing that poor reading skills are fundamentally linked to other social problems—including poverty, drug abuse, and homelessness—she spends much of her time drawing attention to the need for better reading skills. In 1989, she announced the creation of the Barbara Bush Foundation for Family Literacy to establish literacy as a goal for all American families and support programs to promote reading.

Mrs. Bush encourages volunteer work by all Americans. She works as a volunteer to help many groups, including single parents and AIDS victims. She has made unpublicized visits to homeless shelters to learn firsthand the problems that have put people there.

On the south lawn President Bush gives a hurried interview as he leaves for Camp David in December 1990, during the Persian Gulf crisis. In addition to regular press conferences, such encounters allow reporters to question the President on topics of national interest.

Y ET, DESPITE all the support a President may receive from his wife and from his advisers, nothing can relieve him of the sole responsibility of making the nation's ultimate decisions. With word and act, he marks his place in history when he signs or vetoes a bill on economic affairs, for instance; when he proposes a foreign-aid program; or issues an executive order for military operations abroad.

The more forceful the President, the more distinct his image. Cartoons of Teddy Roosevelt, for one, with his toothy grin and round glasses, evoke the earnest conservationist who helped preserve the nation's natural resources, and the indomitable David who fought the Goliaths of industrial monopoly.

The weight of the President's obligations is never so starkly displayed, however, as when his decision alone sets his country on a path of life or death, peace or war. Facing such a challenge, McKinley wept, said a confidant, in pouring out his troubles in the Red Room during the frantic days before the Spanish-American War. Wilson's call for a declaration of war against Germany followed sleepless nights of assessing the consequences. After Truman took the awesome responsibility of the atomic bombing of Japan in World War II, he wrote in his autobiography that he "regarded the bomb as a military weapon and never had any doubt that it should be used."

As the weapons of war grew ever more nightmarish, there came the perilous week in 1962 when the United States and the Soviet Union stood "eyeball to eyeball," H-bombs ready. President Kennedy had made his irrevocable decision to block Soviet ships from bringing more ballistic missiles to Cuba. Until the Soviet Union backed off, the world's future wavered in the balance.

Ten years later, an unprecedented domestic crisis cast its first dark shadow across the Nixon White House with news of a break-in at the offices of the Democratic National Committee in the Capital. Linked with the Republican Committee to Re-elect the President, the seemingly

minor incident grew into a series of investigations and criminal indictments that resulted in President Nixon's resignation in the face of almost certain impeachment.

Though such moments of high drama are mercifully rare in White House history, every President deals from time to time with international tensions that may carry the spark of potential explosion.

Early in September 1978 President Carter initiated a series of meetings at Camp David that brought together President Sadat of Egypt and Prime Minister Begin of Israel. As a result of intense three-way discussions, Carter achieved a history-making accord between the two countries.

President Reagan found the tinderbox in the Middle East and terrorism elsewhere in the world continuing threats to peace. However, two summit meetings with Soviet leader Gorbachev initiated a useful dialogue on arms limitation and nuclear proliferation.

Alone in the Oval Office President Bush works at his desk. Memos from his staff and Cabinet, on subjects that influence events in the United States and around the world, take priority—as Millie waits patiently.

P RESIDENT BUSH faced a crisis of enormous magnitude in August 1990, when Saddam Hussein, dictator of Iraq, invaded Kuwait. The move threatened Saudi Arabia and endangered vital U. S. interests in the area. Declaring that Iraq's aggression "will not stand," President Bush ordered U. S. troops to Saudi Arabia. The President called this deployment and later buildup "Operation Desert Shield."

At the same time, the President led initiatives for U.N. Security Council resolutions imposing economic sanctions on Iraq to force a withdrawal. As aggression continued, on November 30, the U.N. Security Council adopted a further resolution to use force, if necessary, to liberate Kuwait; it gave Saddam a January 15 deadline to withdraw his army. On January 12, 1991, Congress authorized the President to wage war to expel Iraq's armed forces from Kuwait. The deadline passed without compliance, and Operation Desert Shield erupted into Operation Desert Storm. War had begun.

After weeks of heavy allied bombing, the United States led forces in a ground war that routed the Iraqis from Kuwait with minimal allied losses. Yet President Bush's expectation of an Iraqi overthrow of Saddam was not realized and peace in the area remains elusive.

Back on the home front, the President has faced problems of a weakened U. S. economy and ongoing recession. He has also differed with Congress on many domestic issues. One bright exception was the signing of the 1990 Clean Air Act on November 15. It restricted pollutants causing acid rain and other problems.

Solutions to wars and economic problems will always be hard to find. However, between the great events of crisis and celebration, most Americans tend to regard their White House as a serene place—one that is usually glamorous and yet always attainable by an ambitious citizen.

On one occasion, a visitor ended a public tour of the mansion in company with a boy about nine years old. The boy, she reported, looked back at the big white building shining in the sun.

"I'm going to live here," he said confidently, "when I grow up."

INDEX

Boldface indicates illustrations; *italic* refers to picture legends (captions)

Composition for THE LIVING WHITE HOUSE by the Typographic section of National Geographic Production Services, Pre-Press Division. Printed and bound by R. R. Donnelley & Sons Co., Willard, Ohio. Color separations by Graphic Art Service, Nashville, Tenn. Cover and dust jacket printed by Peake Printers, Cheverly, Md.

ENDPAPER: *In the East Room, the Prince of Wales bows at President Buchanan's public reception in 1860.*
LIBRARY OF CONGRESS